for

_____

from

_____

Bible Promises for You from the New International Version
Copyright ©2005 by The Zondervan Corporation.
ISBN 0-310-80388-8
Previously published as *God's Promises for You* from the New
International Version.

Developed and produced by The Livingstone Corporation.

Requests for information should be addressed to:
Inspirio, the gift group of Zondervan
Grand Rapids, Michigan 49530
http://www.inspiriogifts.com
Cover and Interior design: Pamela J. L. Eicher
Printed in China.

17 18 / LPC / 36 35

BIBLE PROMISES *for* YOU

from the
NEW INTERNATIONAL VERSION

inspirio™

TABLE OF CONTENTS

FOREWORD
by Joni Eareckson Tada

In the beginning was the Word, and the Word was with God, and the Word was God.

—John 1:1

The Bible reveals God's soul to us in a way that no other book is able to do. It is history, wisdom, and poetry. It is unparalleled as a compendium of theology, philosophy, and ethics. It is a gospel tract, distilling the essence of our relationship with an eternal God.

Though the Bible contains all these things, it is at its heart an autobiography. The Bible is all about God. Through even the most twisted and unlikely narratives, some even tawdry, we see God's soul reflected to us.

Every word speaks something to us of his soul.

Treasure God's Word today. In everything you read, you will come to know the soul of God, he who is the lover of your soul.

PLAN OF SALVATION
by Billy Graham

The Bible says that we have been separated and alienated from God because we have willfully turned our backs on Him and are determined to run our lives without Him. This is what the Bible means by sin—choosing our way instead of God's way, and not giving Him His rightful place in our lives. The evidence of this is all around us, in the moral chaos and heartache of our world. The headlines scream every day that we live in a broken, sin-ravaged world.

But in addition, the message declares that God still loves us. He yearns to forgive us and bring us back to Himself. He wants to fill our lives with meaning and purpose right now. Then He wants us to spend all eternity with Him in Heaven, free forever from the pain and sorrow and death of this world.

Moreover, God has done everything possible to reconcile us to Himself. He did this in a way that staggers our imagination. In God's plan, by His death on the Cross, Jesus Christ paid the penalty for our sins, taking the judgment of God that we deserve upon Himself when He died on the Cross. Now, by His resurrection from the dead, Christ has broken the bonds of death and opened the way to eternal life for us.

The resurrection also confirms for all time that Jesus was in fact who He said He was: the unique Son of God, sent from Heaven to save us from our sins. Now God freely offers us the gift of forgiveness and eternal life.

Finally, this message is about our response. Like any other gift, God's gift of salvation does not become ours until we accept it and make it our own. God has done everything possible to provide salvation. But we must reach out in faith and accept it.

How do we do this?

First, by confessing to God that we are sinners and in need of His forgiveness; then by repenting of our sins and, with God's help, turning from them.

Second, by committing our lives to Jesus Christ as Lord and Savior. The best-known verse in the New Testament states the Gospel concisely: "For God so loved the world that he gave his one and only Son, that whoever believes in him shall not perish but have eternal life. For God did not send his Son into the world to condemn the world, but to save the world through him" (John 3:16–17). God in His grace invites us to receive His Son into our lives today.

If you have never done so, I invite you to bow your head right now and by a simple prayer of faith open your heart to Jesus Christ. God receives us just as we are. No matter who we are or what we have done, we are saved only because of what Christ has done for us. I will not go to Heaven because I have preached to great crowds. I will go to Heaven for one reason: Jesus Christ died for me, and I am trusting Him alone for my salvation. Christ died for you also, and He freely offers you the gift of eternal life as you commit your life to Him.

When you do, you become a child of God, adopted into His family forever. He also comes to live within you and will begin to change you from within. No one who truly gives his or her life to Christ will ever be the same, for the promise of His Word is true:

"Therefore, if anyone is in Christ, he is a new creation; the old has gone, the new has come! All this is from God, who reconciled us to himself through Christ and gave us the ministry of reconciliation" (2 Corinthians 5:17–18).

We have seen this happen countless times all over the world, and it can happen in your life as well. Open your life to Christ today.

ACCOMPLISHMENT

I have fought the good fight, I have finished the race, I have kept the faith. Now there is in store for me the crown of righteousness, which the Lord, the righteous Judge, will award to me on that day—and not only to me, but also to all who have longed for his appearing.

2 Timothy 4:7–8

I press on to take hold of that for which Christ Jesus took hold of me. Brothers, I do not consider myself yet to have taken hold of it. But one thing I do: Forgetting what is behind and straining toward what is ahead, I press on toward the goal to win the prize for which God has called me heavenward in Christ Jesus. Only let us live up to what we have already attained.

Philippians 3:12–14, 16

Everyone may eat and drink, and find satisfaction in all his toil—this is the gift of God.

Ecclesiastes 3:13

ACCOMPLISHMENT

LORD, you establish peace for us;
   all that we have accomplished you have
     done for us.

Isaiah 26:12

A longing fulfilled is a tree of life.

Proverbs 13:12

Whatever was to my profit I now consider
loss for the sake of Christ. What is more, I
consider everything a loss compared to the
surpassing greatness of knowing Christ Jesus
my Lord, for whose sake I have lost all
things. I consider them rubbish, that I may
gain Christ and be found in him, not having
a righteousness of my own that comes from
the law, but that which is through faith in
Christ—the righteousness that comes from
God and is by faith.

Philippians 3:7–9

You will eat the fruit of your labor;
   blessings and prosperity will be yours.

Psalm 128:2

ANSWERED PRAYER

Jesus said, "In that day you will no longer ask me anything. I tell you the truth, my Father will give you whatever you ask in my name. Until now you have not asked for anything in my name. Ask and you will receive, and your joy will be complete."

John 16:23–24

They will not toil in vain
   or bear children doomed to misfortune;
for they will be a people blessed by the LORD,
   they and their descendants with them.
Before they call I will answer;
   while they are still speaking I will hear.

Isaiah 65:23–24

Jesus said, "Ask and it will be given to you; seek and you will find; knock and the door will be opened to you. For everyone who asks receives; he who seeks finds; and to him who knocks, the door will be opened."

Matthew 7:7–8

ANSWERED PRAYER

In my distress I called to the LORD,
  and he answered me.
From the depths of the grave I called for help,
  and you listened to my cry.

Jonah 2:2

The LORD is near to all who call on him,
  to all who call on him in truth.
He fulfills the desires of those who fear him;
  he hears their cry and saves them.

Psalm 145:18–19

God will respond to the prayer of the destitute;
  he will not despise their plea.
Let this be written for a future generation,
  that a people not yet created may praise the
  LORD.

Psalm 102:17–18

"Call to me and I will answer you and tell
you great and unsearchable things you do
not know," says the LORD.

Jeremiah 33:3

ASSURANCE

Faith is being sure of what we hope for and certain of what we do not see.

Hebrews 11:1

I am convinced that neither death nor life, neither angels nor demons, neither the present nor the future, nor any powers, neither height nor depth, nor anything else in all creation, will be able to separate us from the love of God that is in Christ Jesus our Lord.

Romans 8:38–39

"Though the mountains be shaken
*   and the hills be removed,*
yet my unfailing love for you will not be shaken
*   nor my covenant of peace be removed,"*
*   says the LORD, who has compassion on you.*

Isaiah 54:10

Those who have served well gain an excellent standing and great assurance in their faith in Christ Jesus.

1 Timothy 3:13

ASSURANCE

Jesus said, "My sheep listen to my voice; I know them, and they follow me. I give them eternal life, and they shall never perish; no one can snatch them out of my hand. My Father, who has given them to me, is greater than all; no one can snatch them out of my Father's hand."

John 10:27–29

I am not ashamed, because I know whom I have believed, and am convinced that he is able to guard what I have entrusted to him for that day.

2 Timothy 1:12

Brothers, since we have confidence to enter the Most Holy Place by the blood of Jesus ... let us draw near to God with a sincere heart in full assurance of faith, having our hearts sprinkled to cleanse us from a guilty conscience and having our bodies washed with pure water.

Hebrews 10:19, 22

BELIEF

God so loved the world that he gave his one and only Son, that whoever believes in him shall not perish but have eternal life.

John 3:16

Jesus said, "I tell you the truth, he who believes has everlasting life."

John 6:47

If you confess with your mouth, "Jesus is Lord," and believe in your heart that God raised him from the dead, you will be saved. For it is with your heart that you believe and are justified, and it is with your mouth that you confess and are saved.

Romans 10:9–10

Without faith it is impossible to please God, because anyone who comes to him must believe that he exists and that he rewards those who earnestly seek him.

Hebrews 11:6

Whoever believes in God's Son is not condemned.

John 3:18

BELIEF

They replied, "Believe in the Lord Jesus, and you will be saved—you and your household."

Acts 16:31

All the prophets testify about Jesus of Nazareth that everyone who believes in him receives forgiveness of sins through his name.

Acts 10:43

To all who received him Jesus Christ, to those who believed in his name, he gave the right to become children of God.

John 1:12

Jesus told him, "Because you have seen me, you have believed; blessed are those who have not seen and yet have believed."

John 20:29

Jesus said to her, "I am the resurrection and the life. He who believes in me will live, even though he dies; and whoever lives and believes in me will never die."

John 11:25–26

BLESSINGS

Blessed is the man
  who does not walk in the counsel of the
    wicked
or stand in the way of sinners
  or sit in the seat of mockers.
But his delight is in the law of the LORD,
  and on his law he meditates day and night.

  Psalm 1:1–2

Blessed is the man who trusts in the LORD,
  whose confidence is in him.

  Jeremiah 17:7

Praise be to the God and Father of our
Lord Jesus Christ, who has blessed us in
the heavenly realms with every spiritual
blessing in Christ.

  Ephesians 1:3

How great is your goodness,
  which you have stored up for those who
    fear you,
which you bestow in the sight of men
  on those who take refuge in you.

  Psalm 31:19

BLESSINGS

There is no difference between Jew and Gentile—the same Lord is Lord of all and richly blesses all who call on him, for, "Everyone who calls on the name of the Lord will be saved."

Romans 10:12-13

Every good and perfect gift is from above, coming down from the Father of the heavenly lights, who does not change like shifting shadows.

James 1:17

Blessed are those you choose
  and bring near to live in your courts!
We are filled with the good things of your
    house,
of your holy temple.

Psalm 65:4

Jesus said, "Blessed are the poor in spirit,
  for theirs is the kingdom of heaven."
Matthew 5:3

CHARITY

Blessed is he who is kind to the needy.
Proverbs 14:21

Blessed is he who has regard for the weak;
*   the LORD delivers him in times of trouble.*
The LORD will protect him and preserve his life;
*   he will bless him in the land*
*   and not surrender him to the desire of his foes.*
Psalm 41:1–2

He who gives to the poor will lack nothing,
*   but he who closes his eyes to them*
*   receives many curses.*
Proverbs 28:27

He who is kind to the poor lends to the LORD,
*   and he will reward him for what he has*
*   done.*
Proverbs 19:17

The King will reply, "I tell you the truth,
whatever you did for one of the least of these
brothers of mine, you did for me."
Matthew 25:40

CHARITY

A generous man will prosper;
  he who refreshes others will himself be
    refreshed.

Proverbs 11:25

Jesus said, "If anyone gives even a cup of
cold water to one of these little ones because
he is my disciple, I tell you the truth, he will
certainly not lose his reward."

Matthew 10:42

A generous man will himself be blessed,
  for he shares his food with the poor.

Proverbs 22:9

Jesus said, "When you give a banquet, invite
the poor, the crippled, the lame, the blind,
and you will be blessed. Although they cannot repay you, you will be repaid at the resurrection of the righteous."

Luke 14:13–14

CHILDREN

Sons are a heritage from the LORD,
*   children a reward from him.*
Like arrows in the hands of a warrior
*   are sons born in one's youth.*
Blessed is the man
*   whose quiver is full of them.*

Psalm 127:3–5

Train a child in the way he should go,
*   and when he is old he will not turn from it.*

Proverbs 22:6

Discipline your son, and he will give you
*   peace;*
*   he will bring delight to your soul.*

Proverbs 29:17

I have no greater joy than to hear that my children are walking in the truth.

3 John 1:4

Jesus said, "Whoever humbles himself like this child is the greatest in the kingdom of heaven."

Matthew 18:4

CHILDREN

Fix these words of mine in your hearts and minds; tie them as symbols on your hands and bind them on your foreheads. Teach them to your children, talking about them when you sit at home and when you walk along the road, when you lie down and when you get up. Write them on the doorframes of your houses and on your gates, so that your days and the days of your children may be many in the land that the LORD swore to give your forefathers, as many as the days that the heavens are above the earth.

Deuteronomy 11:18–21

Peter replied, "Repent and be baptized, every one of you, in the name of Jesus Christ for the forgiveness of your sins. And you will receive the gift of the Holy Spirit. The promise is for you and your children and for all who are far off—for all whom the Lord our God will call."

Acts 2:38–39

CHILDREN OF GOD

"I will be a Father to you,
and you will be my sons and daughters,"
says the Lord Almighty.

2 Corinthians 6:18

Because you are sons, God sent the Spirit of his Son into our hearts, the Spirit who calls out, "Abba, Father." So you are no longer a slave, but a son; and since you are a son, God has made you also an heir.

Galatians 4:6–7

Those who are led by the Spirit of God are sons of God. For you did not receive a spirit that makes you a slave again to fear, but you received the Spirit of sonship. And by him we cry, "Abba, Father."

Romans 8:14–15

You are all sons of God through faith in Christ Jesus. There is neither Jew nor Greek, slave nor free, male nor female, for you are all one in Christ Jesus.

Galatians 3:26, 28

CHILDREN OF GOD

How great is the love the Father has lavished on us, that we should be called children of God! And that is what we are! The reason the world does not know us is that it did not know him.

1 John 3:1

Be imitators of God, therefore, as dearly loved children and live a life of love, just as Christ loved us and gave himself up for us as a fragrant offering and sacrifice to God.

Ephesians 5:1–2

The Spirit himself testifies with our spirit that we are God's children.

Romans 8:16

Dear friends, now we are children of God, and what we will be has not yet been made known. But we know that when he appears, we shall be like him, for we shall see him as he is.

1 John 3:2

CHRIST'S RETURN

Christ was sacrificed once to take away the sins of many people; and he will appear a second time, not to bear sin, but to bring salvation to those who are waiting for him.

Hebrews 9:28

Jesus said, "In my Father's house are many rooms; if it were not so, I would have told you. I am going there to prepare a place for you. And if I go and prepare a place for you, I will come back and take you to be with me that you also may be where I am."

John 14:2–3

"Men of Galilee," the men dressed in white said, "why do you stand here looking into the sky? This same Jesus, who has been taken from you into heaven, will come back in the same way you have seen him go into heaven."

Acts 1:11

Look, he is coming with the clouds, and every eye will see him.

Revelation 1:7

CHRIST'S RETURN

The Lord himself will come down from heaven, with a loud command, with the voice of the archangel and with the trumpet call of God, and the dead in Christ will rise first.

1 Thessalonians 4:16

Jesus said, "Behold, I am coming soon! My reward is with me, and I will give to everyone according to what he has done."

Revelation 22:12

The day of the Lord will come like a thief. The heavens will disappear with a roar; the elements will be destroyed by fire, and the earth and everything in it will be laid bare.

2 Peter 3:10

Jesus said, "You also must be ready, because the Son of Man will come at an hour when you do not expect him."

Luke 12:40

Jesus said, "This gospel of the kingdom will be preached in the whole world as a testimony to all nations, and then the end will come."

Matthew 24:14

CHURCH

You are a chosen people, a royal priesthood, a holy nation, a people belonging to God, that you may declare the praises of him who called you out of darkness into his wonderful light.

1 Peter 2:9

God's household ... is the church of the living God, the pillar and foundation of the truth.

1 Timothy 3:15

Christ is the head of the body, the church; he is the beginning and the firstborn from among the dead, so that in everything he might have the supremacy.

Colossians 1:18

Let us not give up meeting together, as some are in the habit of doing, but let us encourage one another—and all the more as you see the Day approaching.

Hebrews 10:25

CHURCH

Let the word of Christ dwell in you richly as you teach and admonish one another with all wisdom, and as you sing psalms, hymns and spiritual songs with gratitude in your hearts to God.

Colossians 3:16

They devoted themselves to the apostles' teaching and to the fellowship, to the breaking of bread and to prayer. Everyone was filled with awe, and many wonders and miraculous signs were done by the apostles. All the believers were together and had everything in common. Selling their possessions and goods, they gave to anyone as he had need. Every day they continued to meet together in the temple courts. They broke bread in their homes and ate together with glad and sincere hearts, praising God and enjoying the favor of all the people. And the Lord added to their number daily those who were being saved.

Acts 2:42–47

COMFORT

Praise be to the God and Father of our Lord
Jesus Christ, the Father of compassion and
the God of all comfort, who comforts us in
all our troubles, so that we can comfort those
in any trouble with the comfort we ourselves
have received from God.

2 Corinthians 1:3–4

The LORD your God is with you,
*   he is mighty to save.*
He will take great delight in you,
*   he will quiet you with his love,*
*   he will rejoice over you with singing.*

Zephaniah 3:17

The LORD is close to the brokenhearted
*   and saves those who are crushed in spirit.*

Psalm 34:18

The Lamb at the center of the throne will
*   be their shepherd;*
*   he will lead them to springs of living water.*
And God will wipe away every tear from
*   their eyes.*

Revelation 7:17

COMFORT

Let the beloved of the LORD rest secure in him,
  for he shields him all day long,
   and the one the LORD loves rests between
     his shoulders.

Deuteronomy 33:12

"I have seen his ways, but I will heal him;
  I will guide him and restore comfort
     to him,
   creating praise on the lips of the mourners
     in Israel.
Peace, peace, to those far and near,"
  says the LORD. "And I will heal them."

Isaiah 57:18–19

"Then maidens will dance and be glad,
  young men and old as well.
I will turn their mourning into gladness;
  I will give them comfort and joy instead
   of sorrow," declares the LORD.

Jeremiah 31:13

COMPASSION

You are a forgiving God, gracious and
compassionate, slow to anger and abounding in love.

Nehemiah 9:17

The LORD *longs to be gracious to you;*
 he rises to show you compassion.
For the LORD *is a God of justice.*
 Blessed are all who wait for him!

Isaiah 30:18

As a father has compassion on his children,
 so the LORD *has compassion on those*
  who fear him.

Psalm 103:13

I will betroth you to me forever;
 I will betroth you in righteousness
  and justice,
 in love and compassion.

Hosea 2:19

COMPASSION

"Though the mountains be shaken
  and the hills be removed,
yet my unfailing love for you will not be
    shaken
  nor my covenant of peace be removed,"
  says the LORD, who has compassion on you.
Isaiah 54:10

Your compassion is great, O LORD;
  preserve my life according to your laws.
Psalm 119:156

Because of the LORD's great love we are
    not consumed,
  for his compassions never fail.
They are new every morning;
  great is your faithfulness.
Lamentations 3:22–23

The LORD is good to all;
  he has compassion on all he has made.
Psalm 145:9

CONFIDENCE

The LORD *will be your confidence*
  and will keep your foot from being snared.
                                    Proverbs 3:26

We say with confidence,
"The Lord is my helper; I will not be afraid.
  What can man do to me?"
                                    Hebrews 13:6

Though an army besiege me,
  my heart will not fear;
though war break out against me,
  even then will I be confident.
                                    Psalm 27:3

Even though I walk
  through the valley of the shadow of death,
I will fear no evil,
  for you are with me;
your rod and your staff,
  they comfort me.
                                    Psalm 23:4

This is the confidence we have in approaching God: that if we ask anything according
to his will, he hears us.
                                    1 John 5:14

CONFIDENCE

We know and rely on the love God has for us. God is love. Whoever lives in love lives in God, and God in him. In this way, love is made complete among us so that we will have confidence on the day of judgment, because in this world we are like him.

1 John 4:16–17

Such confidence as this is ours through Christ before God. Not that we are competent in ourselves to claim anything for ourselves, but our competence comes from God.

2 Corinthians 3:4–5

Dear children, continue in him, so that when he appears we may be confident and unashamed before him at his coming.

1 John 2:28

Let us then approach the throne of grace with confidence, so that we may receive mercy and find grace to help us in our time of need.

Hebrews 4:16

CONTENTMENT

I am not saying this because I am in need,
for I have learned to be content whatever
the circumstances. I know what it is to be in
need, and I know what it is to have plenty. I
have learned the secret of being content in
any and every situation, whether well fed or
hungry, whether living in plenty or in want.
I can do everything through him who gives
me strength.

Philippians 4:11–13

Godliness with contentment is great gain.

1 Timothy 6:6

*Naked I came from my mother's womb,
    and naked I will depart.
The LORD gave and the LORD has taken away;
    may the name of the LORD be praised.*

Job 1:21

Keep your lives free from the love of money
and be content with what you have, because
God has said,

> "Never will I leave you;
>   never will I forsake you."

Hebrews 13:5

CONTENTMENT

The fear of the LORD leads to life:
Then one rests content, untouched by trouble.

Proverbs 19:23

If we have food and clothing, we will be content with that.

1 Timothy 6:8

I said to the LORD, "You are my LORD;
apart from you I have no good thing."

Psalm 16:2

The cheerful heart has a continual feast.

Proverbs 15:15

John answered, "The man with two tunics should share with him who has none, and the one who has food should do the same." Tax collectors also came to be baptized. "Teacher," they asked, "what should we do?" "Don't collect any more than you are required to," he told them. Then some soldiers asked him, "And what should we do?" He replied, "Don't extort money and don't accuse people falsely—be content with your pay."

Luke 3:11–14

COURAGE

Be strong and take heart,
　　all you who hope in the LORD.

Psalm 31:24

When I am afraid,
　　I will trust in you.
In God, whose word I praise,
　　in God I trust; I will not be afraid.

Psalm 56:3–4

"When you pass through the waters,
　　I will be with you;
and when you pass through the rivers,
　　they will not sweep over you.
When you walk through the fire,
　　you will not be burned;
　　the flames will not set you ablaze.
For I am the LORD, your God,
　　the Holy One of Israel, your Savior."

Isaiah 43:2–3

The LORD your God, who is among you, is
a great and awesome God.

Deuteronomy 7:21

COURAGE

Have no fear of sudden disaster
   or of the ruin that overtakes the wicked,
for the LORD will be your confidence
   and will keep your foot from being snared.
Proverbs 3:25–26

"I will strengthen you and help you;
   I will uphold you with my righteous
      right hand," says the LORD.
Isaiah 41:10

The LORD is my light and my salvation—
   whom shall I fear?
The LORD is the stronghold of my life—
   of whom shall I be afraid?
Psalm 27:1

Be strong and courageous. Do not be afraid
or terrified because of them, for the LORD
your God goes with you; he will never leave
you nor forsake you.
Deuteronomy 31:6

DECISIONS

This is what the LORD says:
"Stand at the crossroads and look;
ask for the ancient paths,
ask where the good way is, and walk in it,
and you will find rest for your souls."

Jeremiah 6:16

If any of you lacks wisdom, he should ask God, who gives generously to all without finding fault, and it will be given to him.

James 1:5

"Call to me and I will answer you and tell you great and unsearchable things you do not know," says the LORD.

Jeremiah 33:3

Jesus said, "I will ask the Father, and he will give you another Counselor to be with you forever—the Spirit of truth. The world cannot accept him, because it neither sees him nor knows him. But you know him, for he lives with you and will be in you."

John 14:16–17

DECISIONS

This is what the LORD Almighty says: "Give careful thought to your ways."

Haggai 1:5

Trust in the LORD with all your heart
   and lean not on your own understanding;
in all your ways acknowledge him,
   and he will make your paths straight.

Proverbs 3:5–6

In his heart a man plans his course,
   but the LORD determines his steps.

Proverbs 16:9

Commit your way to the LORD;
   trust in him.

Psalm 37:5

Delight yourself in the LORD
   and he will give you the desires of your
      heart.

Psalm 37:4

DISCERNMENT

Jesus said, "When he, the Spirit of truth, comes, he will guide you into all truth. He will not speak on his own; he will speak only what he hears, and he will tell you what is yet to come."

John 16:13

We are from God, and whoever knows God listens to us; but whoever is not from God does not listen to us. This is how we recognize the Spirit of truth and the spirit of falsehood.

1 John 4:6

Do not believe every spirit, but test the spirits to see whether they are from God, because many false prophets have gone out into the world.

1 John 4:1

Test everything. Hold on to the good. Avoid every kind of evil.

1 Thessalonians 5:21–22

DISCERNMENT

We know that we have come to know him if we obey his commands.

1 John 2:3

The man without the Spirit does not accept the things that come from the Spirit of God, for they are foolishness to him, and he cannot understand them, because they are spiritually discerned. The spiritual man makes judgments about all things, but he himself is not subject to any man's judgment:
*"For who has known the mind of the Lord
    that he may instruct him?"*
But we have the mind of Christ.

1 Corinthians 2:14–16

This is how you can recognize the Spirit of God: Every spirit that acknowledges that Jesus Christ has come in the flesh is from God.

1 John 4:2

DISCIPLESHIP

Jesus said, "Whoever serves me must follow me; and where I am, my servant also will be. My Father will honor the one who serves me."

John 12:26

Jesus said, "All men will know that you are my disciples, if you love one another."

John 13:35

When Jesus spoke again to the people, he said, "I am the light of the world. Whoever follows me will never walk in darkness, but will have the light of life."

John 8:12

If they obey and serve him,
*   they will spend the rest of their days in*
*   prosperity*
*   and their years in contentment.*

Job 36:11

Jesus said, "Whoever has my commands and obeys them, he is the one who loves me. He who loves me will be loved by my Father, and I too will love him and show myself to him."

John 14:21

DISCIPLESHIP

To the Jews who had believed him, Jesus said, "If you hold to my teaching, you are really my disciples."

John 8:31

Jesus said, "This is to my Father's glory, that you bear much fruit, showing yourselves to be my disciples."

John 15:8

Jesus said to his disciples, "If anyone would come after me, he must deny himself and take up his cross and follow me. For whoever wants to save his life will lose it, but whoever loses his life for me will find it."

Matthew 16:24–25

In the presence of God and of Christ Jesus, who will judge the living and the dead, and in view of his appearing and his kingdom, I give you this charge: Preach the Word; be prepared in season and out of season; correct, rebuke and encourage—with great patience and careful instruction.

2 Timothy 4:1–2

ENCOURAGEMENT

May our Lord Jesus Christ himself and God
our Father, who loved us and by his grace
gave us eternal encouragement and good
hope, encourage your hearts and strengthen
you in every good deed and word.

2 Thessalonians 2:16–17

You hear, O LORD, the desire of the afflicted;
you encourage them, and you listen to
their cry.

Psalm 10:17

"I know the plans I have for you," declares the
LORD, "plans to prosper you and not to harm
you, plans to give you hope and a future."

Jeremiah 29:11

Though outwardly we are wasting away, yet
inwardly we are being renewed day by day.

2 Corinthians 4:16

ENCOURAGEMENT

The LORD is good to those whose hope is in him,
   to the one who seeks him;
it is good to wait quietly
   for the salvation of the LORD.
                         Lamentations 3:25–26

The LORD will not reject his people;
   he will never forsake his inheritance.
Judgment will again be founded on
      righteousness,
   and all the upright in heart will follow it.
                         Psalm 94:14–15

Cast your cares on the LORD
   and he will sustain you;
   he will never let the righteous fall.
                         Psalm 55:22

Encourage one another and build each other
up, just as in fact you are doing.
                         1 Thessalonians 5:11

ETERNAL LIFE

The world and its desires pass away, but the man who does the will of God lives forever.

1 John 2:17

The wages of sin is death, but the gift of God is eternal life in Christ Jesus our Lord.

Romans 6:23

Jesus said, "God so loved the world that he gave his one and only Son, that whoever believes in him shall not perish but have eternal life."

John 3:16

This is the testimony: God has given us eternal life, and this life is in his Son. He who has the Son has life; he who does not have the Son of God does not have life.

1 John 5:11–12

Jesus said to her, "I am the resurrection and the life. He who believes in me will live, even though he dies; and whoever lives and believes in me will never die."

John 11:25–26

ETERNAL LIFE

Jesus said, "Whoever believes in the Son has eternal life."

John 3:36

Having been justified by his grace, we might become heirs having the hope of eternal life.

Titus 3:7

Jesus said, "My sheep listen to my voice; I know them, and they follow me. I give them eternal life, and they shall never perish; no one can snatch them out of my hand. My Father, who has given them to me, is greater than all; no one can snatch them out of my Father's hand."

John 10:27–29

Jesus said, "This is eternal life: that they may know you, the only true God, and Jesus Christ, whom you have sent."

John 17:3

FAITH

Faith is being sure of what we hope for and
certain of what we do not see.

Hebrews 11:1

Through Christ you believe in God, who
raised him from the dead and glorified him,
and so your faith and hope are in God.

1 Peter 1:21

Though you have not seen Christ, you love
him; and even though you do not see him
now, you believe in him and are filled with
an inexpressible and glorious joy.

1 Peter 1:8

This is a trustworthy saying that deserves
full acceptance (and for this we labor and
strive), that we have put our hope in the
living God, who is the Savior of all men,
and especially of those who believe.

1 Timothy 4:9–10

May your unfailing love rest upon us, O LORD,
even as we put our hope in you.

Psalm 33:22

FAITH

What does the Scripture say? "Abraham believed God, and it was credited to him as righteousness."

Romans 4:3

Since we have been justified through faith, we have peace with God through our Lord Jesus Christ.

Romans 5:1

Jesus said, "I tell you the truth, anyone who has faith in me will do what I have been doing. He will do even greater things than these, because I am going to the Father."

John 14:12

Jesus said, "I tell you the truth, if you have faith as small as a mustard seed, you can say to this mountain, 'Move from here to there' and it will move. Nothing will be impossible for you."

Matthew 17:20

FAITHFULNESS

Let love and faithfulness never leave you;
>   bind them around your neck,
>   write them on the tablet of your heart.
Then you will win favor and a good name
>   in the sight of God and man.

Proverbs 3:3–4

Love the LORD, all his saints!
>   The LORD preserves the faithful,
>   but the proud he pays back in full.

Psalm 31:23

To the faithful you show yourself faithful,
>   to the blameless you show yourself
>   blameless, O LORD.

2 Samuel 22:26

The LORD loves the just
>   and will not forsake his faithful ones.

Psalm 37:28

FAITHFULNESS

God holds victory in store for the upright,
*   he is a shield to those whose walk is*
*   blameless,*
for he guards the course of the just
*   and protects the way of his faithful ones.*
*   Proverbs 2:7–8*

Those who plan what is good find love and
*   faithfulness.*
*   Proverbs 14:22*

Jesus said, "Be faithful, even to the point of
death, and I will give you the crown of life."
*   Revelation 2:10*

If anyone is to go into captivity,
*   into captivity he will go.*
If anyone is to be killed with the sword,
*   with the sword he will be killed.*
This calls for patient endurance and faithfulness on the part of the saints.
*   Revelation 13:10*

FAITHFULNESS OF GOD

God, who has called you into fellowship with
his Son Jesus Christ our Lord, is faithful.

1 Corinthians 1:9

The LORD is good and his love endures
        forever;
    his faithfulness continues through all
        generations.

Psalm 100:5

"Though the mountains be shaken
    and the hills be removed,
yet my unfailing love for you will not be shaken
    nor my covenant of peace be removed,"
    says the LORD, who has compassion on you.

Isaiah 54:10

Because of the LORD'S great love we are not
        consumed,
    for his compassions never fail.
They are new every morning;
    great is your faithfulness.

Lamentations 3:22–23

FAITHFULNESS OF GOD

The works of his hands are faithful and just;
all his precepts are trustworthy.
They are steadfast for ever and ever,
done in faithfulness and uprightness.
Psalm 111:7–8

Know therefore that the LORD your God is
God; he is the faithful God, keeping his
covenant of love to a thousand generations of
those who love him and keep his commands.
Deuteronomy 7:9

If we confess our sins, he is faithful and just
and will forgive us our sins and purify us
from all unrighteousness.
1 John 1:9

Great is your love, higher than the heavens;
your faithfulness reaches to the skies.
Psalm 108:4

The Lord is faithful, and he will strengthen
and protect you from the evil one.
2 Thessalonians 3:3

FINANCES

Jesus said to them, "Watch out! Be on your guard against all kinds of greed; a man's life does not consist in the abundance of his possessions."

Luke 12:15

Keep your lives free from the love of money and be content with what you have, because God has said,
"Never will I leave you;
   never will I forsake you."

Hebrews 13:5

Jesus said, "Whoever can be trusted with very little can also be trusted with much, and whoever is dishonest with very little will also be dishonest with much."

Luke 16:10

Honor the LORD with your wealth,
   with the firstfruits of all your crops;
then your barns will be filled to overflowing,
   and your vats will brim over with
      new wine.

Proverbs 3:9–10

FINANCES

"Bring the whole tithe into the storehouse, that there may be food in my house. Test me in this," says the LORD Almighty, "and see if I will not throw open the floodgates of heaven and pour out so much blessing that you will not have room enough for it."

Malachi 3:10

My God will meet all your needs according to his glorious riches in Christ Jesus.

Philippians 4:19

If there is a poor man among your brothers in any of the towns of the land that the LORD your God is giving you, do not be hardhearted or tightfisted toward your poor brother. Rather be openhanded and freely lend him whatever he needs.

Deuteronomy 15:7–8

Let no debt remain outstanding, except the continuing debt to love one another, for he who loves his fellowman has fulfilled the law.

Romans 13:8

FINANCES

Jesus said, "So do not worry, saying, 'What shall we eat?' or 'What shall we drink?' or 'What shall we wear?' For the pagans run after all these things, and your heavenly Father knows that you need them. But seek first his kingdom and his righteousness, and all these things will be given to you as well."

Matthew 6:31–33

He who gathers money little by little makes it grow.

Proverbs 13:11

Give generously to your needy brother and do so without a grudging heart; then because of this the LORD your God will bless you in all your work and in everything you put your hand to.

Deuteronomy 15:10

FINANCES

A good man leaves an inheritance for his
   children's children,
   but a sinner's wealth is stored up for the
   righteous.

Proverbs 13:22

Jesus said, "When you give to the needy,
do not announce it with trumpets, as the
hypocrites do in the synagogues and on the
streets, to be honored by men. I tell you
the truth, they have received their reward
in full. But when you give to the needy, do
not let your left hand know what your
right hand is doing, so that your giving may
be in secret. Then your Father, who sees
what is done in secret, will reward you."

Matthew 6:2–4

FORGIVENESS OF GOD

Peter replied, "Repent and be baptized, every one of you, in the name of Jesus Christ for the forgiveness of your sins. And you will receive the gift of the Holy Spirit."

Acts 2:38

There is now no condemnation for those who are in Christ Jesus, because through Christ Jesus the law of the Spirit of life set me free from the law of sin and death.

Romans 8:1–2

In Jesus we have redemption through his blood, the forgiveness of sins, in accordance with the riches of God's grace.

Ephesians 1:7

When you were dead in your sins and in the uncircumcision of your sinful nature, God made you alive with Christ. He forgave us all our sins, having canceled the written code, with its regulations, that was against us and that stood opposed to us; he took it away, nailing it to the cross.

Colossians 2:13-14

FORGIVENESS OF GOD

You are a forgiving God, gracious and compassionate, slow to anger and abounding in love.

Nehemiah 9:17

If we confess our sins, he is faithful and just and will forgive us our sins and purify us from all unrighteousness.

1 John 1:9

Jesus said, "If you forgive men when they sin against you, your heavenly Father will also forgive you."

Matthew 6:14

As far as the east is from the west,
so far has he removed our transgressions
from us.

Psalm 103:12

I acknowledged my sin to you
and did not cover up my iniquity.
I said, "I will confess
my transgressions to the LORD"—
and you forgave the
guilt of my sin.

Psalm 32:5

FREEDOM

The Spirit of the Sovereign LORD *is on me,*
  because the LORD *has anointed me*
  to preach good news to the poor.
He has sent me to bind up the brokenhearted,
  to proclaim freedom for the captives
  and release from darkness for the prisoners.
                                    Isaiah 61:1

Now that you have been set free from sin
and have become slaves to God, the benefit
you reap leads to holiness, and the result is
eternal life.

                                    Romans 6:22

The creation itself will be liberated from its
bondage to decay and brought into the glorious freedom of the children of God.

                                    Romans 8:21

Jesus said, "If the Son sets you free, you will
be free indeed."

                                    John 8:36

The Lord is the Spirit, and where the Spirit
of the Lord is, there is freedom.

                                    2 Corinthians 3:17

FREEDOM

Through Christ Jesus the law of the Spirit of life set me free from the law of sin and death.

Romans 8:2

"For you who revere my name, the sun of righteousness will rise with healing in its wings. And you will go out and leap like calves released from the stall," says the LORD Almighty.

Malachi 4:2

Jesus said, "If you hold to my teaching, you are really my disciples. Then you will know the truth, and the truth will set you free."

John 8:31–32

It is for freedom that Christ has set us free. Stand firm, then, and do not let yourselves be burdened again by a yoke of slavery.

Galatians 5:1

By dying to what once bound us, we have been released from the law so that we serve in the new way of the Spirit, and not in the old way of the written code.

Romans 7:6

FRIENDSHIP

A *friend loves at all times,*
and a brother is born for adversity.
Proverbs 17:17

Be devoted to one another in brotherly love.
Honor one another above yourselves.
Romans 12:10

Jesus said, "Greater love has no one than
this, that he lay down his life for his friends."
John 15:13

Two are better than one,
because they have a good return for
their work:
If one falls down,
his friend can help him up.
But pity the man who falls
and has no one to help him up!
Ecclesiastes 4:9–10

FRIENDSHIP

A man of many companions may come to
  ruin,
    but there is a friend who sticks closer than
    a brother.

Proverbs 18:24

He who walks with the wise grows wise,
    but a companion of fools suffers harm.

Proverbs 13:20

As iron sharpens iron,
    so one man sharpens another.

Proverbs 27:17

Wounds from a friend can be trusted,
    but an enemy multiplies kisses.

Proverbs 27:6

How good and pleasant it is
    when brothers live together in unity!

Psalm 133:1

FRIENDSHIP OF GOD

Jesus said, "Here I am! I stand at the door and knock. If anyone hears my voice and opens the door, I will come in and eat with him, and he with me."

Revelation 3:20

Jesus replied, "If anyone loves me, he will obey my teaching. My Father will love him, and we will come to him and make our home with him."

John 14:23

The scripture was fulfilled that says, "Abraham believed God, and it was credited to him as righteousness," and he was called God's friend.

James 2:23

Jesus said, "I no longer call you servants, because a servant does not know his master's business. Instead, I have called you friends, for everything that I learned from my Father I have made known to you."

John 15:15

FRIENDSHIP OF GOD

God, who has called you into fellowship with his Son Jesus Christ our Lord, is faithful.

1 Corinthians 1:9

We proclaim to you what we have seen and heard, so that you also may have fellowship with us. And our fellowship is with the Father and with his Son, Jesus Christ.

1 John 1:3

"I led them with cords of human kindness,
with ties of love;
I lifted the yoke from their neck
and bent down to feed them," declares
the LORD.

Hosea 11:4

Cast all your anxiety on him because he cares for you.

1 Peter 5:7

You understand, O LORD;
remember me and care for me.

Jeremiah 15:15

FUTURE

As it is written:
"*No eye has seen,*
  no ear has heard,
no mind has conceived
  what God has prepared for those who
    love him"—
but God has revealed it to us by his Spirit.
The Spirit searches all things, even the deep
things of God.

1 Corinthians 2:9–10

Our citizenship is in heaven. And we eagerly
await a Savior from there, the Lord Jesus
Christ, who, by the power that enables him
to bring everything under his control, will
transform our lowly bodies so that they will
be like his glorious body.

Philippians 3:20–21

Listen, I tell you a mystery: We will not all
sleep, but we will all be changed—in a flash,
in the twinkling of an eye, at the last trumpet.
For the trumpet will sound, the dead will be
raised imperishable, and we will be changed.

1 Corinthians 15:51–52

FUTURE

We are children of God, and what we will be has not yet been made known. But we know that when he appears, we shall be like him, for we shall see him as he is.

1 John 3:2

"I know the plans I have for you," declares the LORD, "plans to prosper you and not to harm you, plans to give you hope and a future."

Jeremiah 29:11

The plans of the LORD stand firm forever,
the purposes of his heart through all
generations.

Psalm 33:11

Why, you do not even know what will happen tomorrow. What is your life? You are a mist that appears for a little while and then vanishes. Instead, you ought to say, "If it is the Lord's will, we will live and do this or that."

James 4:14–15

GIVING

Each man should give what he has decided
in his heart to give, not reluctantly or under
compulsion, for God loves a cheerful giver.

2 Corinthians 9:7

Jesus said, "Give, and it will be given to you.
A good measure, pressed down, shaken
together and running over, will be poured
into your lap. For with the measure you use,
it will be measured to you."

Luke 6:38

Good will come to him who is generous and
    lends freely,
  who conducts his affairs with justice.

Psalm 112:5

A generous man will prosper;
  he who refreshes others will himself be
    refreshed.

Proverbs 11:25

GIVING

A generous man will himself be blessed,
  for he shares his food with the poor.
Proverbs 22:9

Jesus said, "When you give to the needy, do
not let your left hand know what your right
hand is doing, so that your giving may be in
secret. Then your Father, who sees what is
done in secret, will reward you."
Matthew 6:3–4

If your enemy is hungry, give him food to eat;
  he is thirsty, give him water to drink.
Proverbs 25:21

He who gives to the poor will lack nothing,
  but he who closes his eyes to them
  receives many curses.
Proverbs 28:27

GOALS

We make it our goal to please him, whether we are at home in the body or away from it.

2 Corinthians 5:9

Jesus said, "Seek first his kingdom and his righteousness, and all these things will be given to you as well."

Matthew 6:33

Do you not know that in a race all the runners run, but only one gets the prize? Run in such a way as to get the prize.

1 Corinthians 9:24

Brothers, I do not consider myself yet to have taken hold of it. But one thing I do: Forgetting what is behind and straining toward what is ahead, I press on toward the goal to win the prize for which God has called me heavenward in Christ Jesus.

Philippians 3:13–14

GOALS

Do your best to present yourself to God as one approved, a workman who does not need to be ashamed and who correctly handles the word of truth.

2 Timothy 2:15

As God's chosen people, holy and dearly loved, clothe yourselves with compassion, kindness, humility, gentleness and patience.

Colossians 3:12

In your hearts set apart Christ as Lord. Always be prepared to give an answer to everyone who asks you to give the reason for the hope that you have. But do this with gentleness and respect.

1 Peter 3:15

Since you are eager to have spiritual gifts, try to excel in gifts that build up the church.

1 Corinthians 14:12

Make it your ambition to lead a quiet life, to mind your own business and to work with your hands, just as we told you.

1 Thessalonians 4:11

GOODNESS OF GOD

The LORD is good to all;
    he has compassion on all he has made.

Psalm 145:9

Good and upright is the LORD;
    therefore he instructs sinners in his ways.

Psalm 25:8

The LORD is good,
    a refuge in times of trouble.
He cares for those who trust in him.

Nahum 1:7

How great is your goodness,
    which you have stored up for those who
        fear you,
which you bestow in the sight of men
    on those who take refuge in you.

Psalm 31:19

The LORD is good to those whose hope is in him,
    to the one who seeks him.

Lamentations 3:25

GOODNESS OF GOD

I am still confident of this:
  I will see the goodness of the LORD
    in the land of the living.

Psalm 27:13

God's divine power has given us everything
we need for life and godliness through our
knowledge of him who called us by his own
glory and goodness.

2 Peter 1:3

I said to the LORD, "You are my LORD;
  apart from you I have no good thing."

Psalm 16:2

We know that in all things God works for
the good of those who love him, who have
been called according to his purpose.

Romans 8:28

GRACE

God raised us up with Christ and seated us
with him in the heavenly realms in Christ
Jesus, in order that in the coming ages he
might show the incomparable riches of his
grace, expressed in his kindness to us in
Christ Jesus.

Ephesians 2:6–7

It is by grace you have been saved, through
faith—and this not from yourselves, it is the
gift of God—not by works, so that no one
can boast. For we are God's workmanship,
created in Christ Jesus to do good works,
which God prepared in advance for us to do.

Ephesians 2:8–10

You know the grace of our Lord Jesus Christ,
that though he was rich, yet for your sakes
he became poor, so that you through his
poverty might become rich.

2 Corinthians 8:9

GUIDANCE

*The L*ORD *will guide you always;*
he will satisfy your needs in a sun-
scorched land
and will strengthen your frame.
You will be like a well-watered garden,
like a spring whose waters never fail.
Isaiah 58:11

If I rise on the wings of the dawn,
if I settle on the far side of the sea,
even there your hand will guide me,
your right hand will hold me fast, O God.
Psalm 139:9–10

"I will lead the blind by ways they have not
known,
along unfamiliar paths I will guide them;
I will turn the darkness into light before them
and make the rough places smooth.
These are the things I will do;
*I will not forsake them," says the L*ORD.
Isaiah 42:16

HEALING

"I will heal my people and will let them enjoy abundant peace and security," says the LORD.

Jeremiah 33:6

"I will heal their waywardness
   and love them freely,
   for my anger has turned away from them,"
declares the LORD.

Hosea 14:4

He himself bore our sins in his body on the tree, so that we might die to sins and live for righteousness; by his wounds you have been healed.

1 Peter 2:24

Praise the LORD, O my soul,
   and forget not all his benefits—
who forgives all your sins
   and heals all your diseases.

Psalm 103:2–3

HEALING

❦❦❦

"I will restore you to health
  and heal your wounds,"
declares the LORD,
"because you are called an outcast,
  Zion for whom no one cares."

Jeremiah 30:17

Heal me, O LORD, and I will be healed;
  save me and I will be saved,
  for you are the one I praise.

Jeremiah 17:14

The prayer offered in faith will make the sick
person well; the Lord will raise him up. If he
has sinned, he will be forgiven.... Confess
your sins to each other and pray for each
other so that you may be healed. The prayer
of a righteous man is powerful and effective.

James 5:15–16

O LORD my God, I called to you for help
  and you healed me.

Psalm 30:2

HEAVEN

Jesus said, "In my Father's house are many
rooms; if it were not so, I would have told
you. I am going there to prepare a place for
you. And if I go and prepare a place for you,
I will come back and take you to be with me
that you also may be where I am."

John 14:2-3

God will wipe every tear from their eyes.
There will be no more death or mourning or
crying or pain, for the old order of things has
passed away.

Revelation 21:4

Never again will they hunger;
never again will they thirst.
The sun will not beat upon them,
nor any scorching heat.
For the Lamb at the center of the throne
will be their shepherd;
he will lead them to springs of living water.
And God will wipe away every tear from
their eyes.

Revelation 7:16–17

HEAVEN

Our citizenship is in heaven. And we eagerly await a Savior from there, the Lord Jesus Christ.

Philippians 3:20

I heard what sounded like a great multitude, like the roar of rushing waters and like loud peals of thunder, shouting:
"Hallelujah!
   For our Lord God Almighty reigns."

Revelation 19:6

According to the Lord's own word, we tell you that we who are still alive, who are left till the coming of the Lord, will certainly not precede those who have fallen asleep. For the Lord himself will come down from heaven, with a loud command, with the voice of the archangel and with the trumpet call of God, and the dead in Christ will rise first. After that, we who are still alive and are left will be caught up together with them in the clouds to meet the Lord in the air. And so we will be with the Lord forever. Therefore encourage each other with these words.

1 Thessalonians 4:15–18

HELP

Because Christ himself suffered when he was tempted, he is able to help those who are being tempted.

Hebrews 2:18

God will deliver the needy who cry out,
    the afflicted who have no one to help.

Psalm 72:12

You, O God, do see trouble and grief;
    you consider it to take it in hand.
The victim commits himself to you;
    you are the helper of the fatherless.

Psalm 10:14

Surely the arm of the LORD is not too short
        to save,
    nor his ear too dull to hear.

Isaiah 59:1

God is our refuge and strength,
    an ever-present help in trouble.

Psalm 46:1

HELP

*The L*ORD *is my strength and my shield;*
my heart trusts in him, and I am helped.
My heart leaps for joy
and I will give thanks to him in song.
Psalm 28:7

Praise be to the Lord, to God our Savior,
who daily bears our burdens.
Psalm 68:19

*It is the Sovereign L*ORD *who helps me.*
Who is he that will condemn me?
They will all wear out like a garment;
the moths will eat them up.
Isaiah 50:9

*We wait in hope for the L*ORD*;*
he is our help and our shield.
Psalm 33:20

HOLINESS

May God himself, the God of peace, sanctify you through and through. May your whole spirit, soul and body be kept blameless at the coming of our Lord Jesus Christ.

1 Thessalonians 5:23

Just as God who called you is holy, so be holy in all you do; for it is written: "Be holy, because I am holy."

1 Peter 1:15–16

God did not call us to be impure, but to live a holy life.

1 Thessalonians 4:7

God chose us in him before the creation of the world to be holy and blameless in his sight. In love he predestined us to be adopted as his sons through Jesus Christ, in accordance with his pleasure and will—to the praise of his glorious grace, which he has freely given us in the One he loves.

Ephesians 1:4–6

HOLINESS

Since we have these promises, dear friends, let us purify ourselves from everything that contaminates body and spirit, perfecting holiness out of reverence for God.

2 Corinthians 7:1

Now that you have been set free from sin and have become slaves to God, the benefit you reap leads to holiness, and the result is eternal life.

Romans 6:22

Make every effort to live in peace with all men and to be holy; without holiness no one will see the Lord.

Hebrews 12:14

Blessed are they whose ways are blameless,
who walk according to the law of the LORD.
Psalm 119:1

The righteousness of the blameless makes a
straight way for them,
but the wicked are brought down by their
own wickedness.

Proverbs 11:5

HONESTY

Surely you desire truth in the inner parts;
*   you teach me wisdom in the inmost place.*

Psalm 51:6

Love ... rejoices with the truth.

1 Corinthians 13:6

Stand firm then, with the belt of truth buckled around your waist, with the breastplate of righteousness in place.

Ephesians 6:14

Whoever of you loves life
*   and desires to see many good days,*
keep your tongue from evil
*   and your lips from speaking lies.*

Psalm 34:12–13

The man of integrity walks securely,
*   but he who takes crooked paths will be*
*   found out.*

Proverbs 10:9

HONESTY

The righteous hate what is false.

Proverbs 13:5

He whose walk is blameless
    and who does what is righteous,
who speaks the truth from his heart.
He who does these things
    will never be shaken.

Psalm 15:2, 5

He who walks righteously
    and speaks what is right …
this is the man who will dwell on the heights,
    whose refuge will be the mountain fortress.
His bread will be supplied,
    and water will not fail him.

Isaiah 33:15–16

An honest answer
    is like a kiss on the lips.

Proverbs 24:26

HOPE

This is a trustworthy saying that deserves full acceptance (and for this we labor and strive), that we have put our hope in the living God, who is the Savior of all men, and especially of those who believe.

1 Timothy 4:9–10

My heart is glad and my tongue rejoices;
my body also will live in hope,
because you will not abandon me to the grave,
nor will you let your Holy One see decay.

Acts 2:26–27

This I call to mind
and therefore I have hope:
Because of the LORD's great love
we are not consumed,
for his compassions never fail.

Lamentations 3:21–22

HOPE

The LORD delights in those who fear him,
  who put their hope in his unfailing love.
Psalm 147:11

Those who hope in the LORD
  will renew their strength.
They will soar on wings like eagles;
  they will run and not grow weary,
  they will walk and not be faint.
Isaiah 40:31

Why are you downcast, O my soul?
  Why so disturbed within me?
Put your hope in God,
  for I will yet praise him,
  my Savior and my God.
Psalm 42:5

May the God of hope fill you with all joy
and peace as you trust in him, so that you
may overflow with hope by the power of the
Holy Spirit.
Romans 15:13

HUMILITY

*Humility and the fear of the LORD
bring wealth and honor and life.*

Proverbs 22:4

Humble yourselves before the Lord, and he
will lift you up.

James 4:10

*The LORD takes delight in his people;
he crowns the humble with salvation.*

Psalm 149:4

*The fear of the LORD teaches a man wisdom,
and humility comes before honor.*

Proverbs 15:33

*The LORD sustains the humble
but casts the wicked to the ground.*

Psalm 147:6

Jesus said, "Whoever humbles himself like
this child is the greatest in the kingdom of
heaven."

Matthew 18:4

HUMILITY

———— ⬦⬦⬦⬦ ————

*The LORD guides the humble in what is right
and teaches them his way.*

Psalm 25:9

Jesus said, "The greatest among you will be
your servant. For whoever exalts himself will
be humbled, and whoever humbles himself
will be exalted."

Matthew 23:11–12

Do nothing out of selfish ambition or vain
conceit, but in humility consider others better than yourselves.

Philippians 2:3

Remind the people to be subject to rulers
and authorities, to be obedient, to be ready
to do whatever is good, to slander no one, to
be peaceable and considerate, and to show
true humility toward all men.

Titus 3:1–2

IDENTITY

Now, this is what the LORD says—
he who created you, O Jacob,
he who formed you, O Israel:
"Fear not, for I have redeemed you;
I have summoned you by name;
you are mine."

Isaiah 43:1

Know that the LORD is God.
It is he who made us, and we are his;
we are his people, the sheep of his pasture.

Psalm 100:3

For the sake of his great name the LORD will not reject his people, because the LORD was pleased to make you his own.

1 Samuel 12:22

You are a chosen people, a royal priesthood, a holy nation, a people belonging to God, that you may declare the praises of him who called you out of darkness into his wonderful light.

1 Peter 2:9

IDENTITY

Come, let us bow down in worship,
    let us kneel before the LORD our Maker;
for he is our God
    and we are the people of his pasture,
    the flock under his care.

Psalm 95:6–7

You also were included in Christ when you
heard the word of truth, the gospel of your
salvation. Having believed, you were marked
in him with a seal, the promised Holy Spirit.

Ephesians 1:13

We are God's workmanship, created in
Christ Jesus to do good works, which God
prepared in advance for us to do.

Ephesians 2:10

As God's chosen people, holy and dearly
loved, clothe yourselves with compassion,
kindness, humility, gentleness and patience.

Colossians 3:12

INTEGRITY

I know, my God, that you test the heart and
are pleased with integrity.

1 Chronicles 29:17

The LORD God is a sun and shield;
  the LORD bestows favor and honor;
no good thing does he withhold
  from those whose walk is blameless.

Psalm 84:11

God holds victory in store for the upright,
  he is a shield to those whose walk is
    blameless,
for he guards the course of the just
  and protects the way of his faithful ones.

Proverbs 2:7–8

The man of integrity walks securely,
  but he who takes crooked paths will be
    found out.

Proverbs 10:9

INTEGRITY

The integrity of the upright guides them,
*   but the unfaithful are destroyed by their*
*   duplicity.*

Proverbs 11:3

In my integrity you uphold me
*   and set me in your presence forever.*

Psalm 41:12

Those who walk uprightly
*   enter into peace;*
*   they find rest as they lie in death.*

Isaiah 57:2

When a man's ways are pleasing to the LORD,
*   he makes even his enemies live at peace*
*   with him.*

Proverbs 16:7

Someone will say, "You have faith; I have
deeds." Show me your faith without deeds,
and I will show you my faith by what I do.

James 2:18

JOY

*You have loved righteousness and hated
       wickedness;
   therefore God, your God, has set you
       above your companions
   by anointing you with the oil of joy.*

Hebrews 1:9

*God will yet fill your mouth with laughter
   and your lips with shouts of joy.*

Job 8:21

*You make me glad by your deeds, O LORD;
   I sing for joy at the works of your hands.*

Psalm 92:4

Though you have not seen him, you love
him; and even though you do not see him
now, you believe in him and are filled with
an inexpressible and glorious joy, for you are
receiving the goal of your faith, the salvation
of your souls.

1 Peter 1:8–9

JOY

Consider it pure joy, my brothers, whenever you face trials of many kinds, because you know that the testing of your faith develops perseverance.

James 1:2–3

Jesus said, "Until now you have not asked for anything in my name. Ask and you will receive, and your joy will be complete."

John 16:24

Therefore my heart is glad and my tongue
*   rejoices;*
*   my body also will live in hope,*
because you will not abandon me to the grave,
*   nor will you let your Holy One see decay.*
You have made known to me the paths of life;
*   you will fill me with joy in your presence.*

Acts 2:26–28

LIFE

Jesus declared, "I am the bread of life. He who comes to me will never go hungry, and he who believes in me will never be thirsty."

John 6:35

Set your hearts on things above, where Christ is seated at the right hand of God. Set your minds on things above, not on earthly things. For you died, and your life is now hidden with Christ in God. When Christ, who is your life, appears, then you also will appear with him in glory.

Colossians 3:1–4

Count yourselves dead to sin but alive to God in Christ Jesus.

Romans 6:11

Through Christ Jesus the law of the Spirit of life set me free from the law of sin and death.

Romans 8:2

LIFE

Jesus said, "The Spirit gives life; the flesh counts for nothing. The words I have spoken to you are spirit and they are life."

John 6:63

If the Spirit of him who raised Jesus from the dead is living in you, he who raised Christ from the dead will also give life to your mortal bodies through his Spirit, who lives in you.

Romans 8:11

The Spirit of God has made me;
  the breath of the Almighty gives me life.

Job 33:4

You have made known to me the paths of life;
  you will fill me with joy in your presence.

Acts 2:28

My son, do not forget my teaching,
  but keep my commands in your heart,
for they will prolong your life many years
  and bring you prosperity.

Proverbs 3:1–2

LOVE FOR GOD

"The most important commandment," answered Jesus, "is this: 'Hear, O Israel, the Lord our God, the Lord is one. Love the Lord your God with all your heart and with all your soul and with all your mind and with all your strength.' The second is this: 'Love your neighbor as yourself.' There is no commandment greater than these."

Mark 12:29–31

Love the LORD your God, listen to his voice, and hold fast to him. For the LORD is your life.

Deuteronomy 30:20

This is love for God: to obey his commands. And his commands are not burdensome.

1 John 5:3

LOVE FOR GOD

Jesus said, "Whoever has my commands and obeys them, he is the one who loves me. He who loves me will be loved by my Father, and I too will love him and show myself to him."

John 14:21

Love the LORD, *all his saints!*
  The LORD preserves the faithful,
  but the proud he pays back in full.

Psalm 31:23

Jesus replied, "If anyone loves me, he will obey my teaching. My Father will love him, and we will come to him and make our home with him."

John 14:23

Anyone who does not love his brother, whom he has seen, cannot love God, whom he has not seen. And he has given us this command: Whoever loves God must also love his brother.

1 John 4:20–21

LOVE FOR OTHERS

If you really keep the royal law found in Scripture, "Love your neighbor as yourself," you are doing right.

James 2:8

We love because he first loved us.

1 John 4:19

Dear friends, let us love one another, for love comes from God. Everyone who loves has been born of God and knows God.

1 John 4:7

As God's chosen people, holy and dearly loved, clothe yourselves with compassion, kindness, humility, gentleness and patience. Bear with each other and forgive whatever grievances you may have against one another. Forgive as the Lord forgave you. And over all these virtues put on love, which binds them all together in perfect unity.

Colossians 3:12–14

Love each other deeply, because love covers over a multitude of sins.

1 Peter 4:8

LOVE FOR OTHERS

No one has ever seen God; but if we love one another, God lives in us and his love is made complete in us.

1 John 4:12

In humility consider others better than yourselves. Each of you should look not only to your own interests, but also to the interests of others.

Philippians 2:3–4

Whoever loves his brother lives in the light, and there is nothing in him to make him stumble.

1 John 2:10

Jesus said, "I tell you: Love your enemies and pray for those who persecute you, that you may be sons of your Father in heaven."

Matthew 5:44-45

He who covers over an offense promotes love, but whoever repeats the matter separates close friends.

Proverbs 17:9

LOVE OF GOD

The LORD *is gracious and compassionate,*
slow to anger and rich in love.

Psalm 145:8

This is love: not that we loved God, but that
he loved us and sent his Son as an atoning
sacrifice for our sins.

1 John 4:10

The Lord appeared to us in the past, saying:
"I have loved you with an everlasting love;
I have drawn you with loving-kindness."

Jeremiah 31:3

As a bridegroom rejoices over his bride,
so will your God rejoice over you.

Isaiah 62:5

Jesus said, "The Father himself loves you
because you have loved me and have
believed that I came from God."

John 16:27

LOVE OF GOD

From everlasting to everlasting
    the LORD's love is with those who fear him,
    and his righteousness with their children's
      children.

Psalm 103:17

The LORD declares, "I will betroth you to
me forever;
    I will betroth you in righteousness
      and justice,
    in love and compassion.
I will betroth you in faithfulness,
    and you will acknowledge the LORD."

Hosea 2:19–20

Because of his great love for us, God, who is
rich in mercy, made us alive with Christ
even when we were dead in transgressions—
it is by grace you have been saved.

Ephesians 2:4–5

MATURITY

Like newborn babies, crave pure spiritual milk, so that by it you may grow up in your salvation.

1 Peter 2:2

Instruct a wise man and he will be wiser still;
teach a righteous man and he will add to
his learning.

Proverbs 9:9

Teach us to number our days aright,
that we may gain a heart of wisdom.

Psalm 90:12

Anyone who lives on milk, being still an infant, is not acquainted with the teaching about righteousness. But solid food is for the mature, who by constant use have trained themselves to distinguish good from evil.

Hebrews 5:13–14

MATURITY

Let us leave the elementary teachings about Christ and go on to maturity.

Hebrews 6:1

Perseverance must finish its work so that you may be mature and complete, not lacking anything.

James 1:4

It was Christ who gave some to be apostles, some to be prophets, some to be evangelists, and some to be pastors and teachers, to prepare God's people for works of service, so that the body of Christ may be built up until we all reach unity in the faith and in the knowledge of the Son of God and become mature, attaining to the whole measure of the fullness of Christ.

Ephesians 4:11–13

God who began a good work in you will carry it on to completion until the day of Christ Jesus.

Philippians 1:6

MEDITATION

Oh, how I love your law!
  I meditate on it all day long.
Psalm 119:97

Blessed is the man
  who does not walk in the counsel of the
    wicked
or stand in the way of sinners
  or sit in the seat of mockers.
But his delight is in the law of the LORD,
  and on his law he meditates day and night.
Psalm 1:1–2

Do not let this Book of the Law depart from your mouth; meditate on it day and night, so that you may be careful to do everything written in it. Then you will be prosperous and successful.

Joshua 1:8

I rise before dawn and cry for help;
  I have put my hope in your word.
My eyes stay open through the watches
    of the night,
  that I may meditate on your promises.
Psalm 119:147–148

MEDITATION

Within your temple, O God,
*   we meditate on your unfailing love.*

Psalm 48:9

I meditate on your precepts
*   and consider your ways.*

Psalm 119:15

I will meditate on all your works
*   and consider all your mighty deeds.*

Psalm 77:12

I will sing to the LORD all my life;
*   I will sing praise to my God as long as I*
*   live.*
May my meditation be pleasing to him,
*   as I rejoice in the LORD.*

Psalm 104:33–34

May the words of my mouth and the
*   meditation of my heart*
*   be pleasing in your sight,*
O LORD, my Rock and my Redeemer.

Psalm 19:14

MERCY OF GOD

The Lord is full of compassion and mercy.
James 5:11

The LORD is gracious and compassionate,
    slow to anger and rich in love.
Psalm 145:8

Seek the LORD while he may be found;
    call on him while he is near.
Let the wicked forsake his way
    and the evil man his thoughts.
Let him turn to the LORD, and he will have
        mercy on him,
    and to our God, for he will freely pardon.
Isaiah 55:6–7

God saved us, not because of righteous
things we had done, but because of his
mercy. He saved us through the washing of
rebirth and renewal by the Holy Spirit.
Titus 3:5

His mercy extends to those who fear him,
    from generation to generation.
Luke 1:50

MERCY OF GOD

The LORD your God is a merciful God; he will not abandon or destroy you or forget the covenant with your forefathers, which he confirmed to them by oath.

Deuteronomy 4:31

The LORD has heard my cry for mercy;
*   the LORD accepts my prayer.*

Psalm 6:9

I, by your great mercy,
*   will come into your house;*
in reverence will I bow down
*   toward your holy temple.*

Psalm 5:7

Who is a God like you,
*   who pardons sin and forgives the*
*   transgression*
*   of the remnant of his inheritance?*
You do not stay angry forever
*   but delight to show mercy.*

Micah 7:18

OBEDIENCE

It is not those who hear the law who are righteous in God's sight, but it is those who obey the law who will be declared righteous.

Romans 2:13

Jesus replied, "Blessed rather are those who hear the word of God and obey it."

Luke 11:28

Jesus said, "Everyone who hears these words of mine and puts them into practice is like a wise man who built his house on the rock. The rain came down, the streams rose, and the winds blew and beat against that house; yet it did not fall, because it had its foundation on the rock."

Matthew 7:24–25

The man who looks intently into the perfect law that gives freedom, and continues to do this, not forgetting what he has heard, but doing it—he will be blessed in what he does.

James 1:25

OBEDIENCE

Jesus said, "Whoever practices and teaches these commands will be called great in the kingdom of heaven."

Matthew 5:19

Jesus said, "If you obey my commands, you will remain in my love, just as I have obeyed my Father's commands and remain in his love. I have told you this so that my joy may be in you and that your joy may be complete."

John 15:10–11

It is the LORD your God you must follow, and him you must revere. Keep his commands and obey him; serve him and hold fast to him.

Deuteronomy 13:4

If anyone obeys his word, God's love is truly made complete in him. This is how we know we are in him: Whoever claims to live in him must walk as Jesus did.

1 John 2:5–6

PARENTS

The righteous man leads a blameless life;
blessed are his children after him.

Proverbs 20:7

Keep God's decrees and commands, which I
am giving you today, so that it may go well
with you and your children after you and
that you may live long in the land the LORD
your God gives you for all time.

Deuteronomy 4:40

Train a child in the way he should go,
and when he is old he will not turn from it.

Proverbs 22:6

Discipline your son, and he will give
you peace;
he will bring delight to your soul.

Proverbs 29:17

The rod of correction imparts wisdom,
but a child left to himself disgraces
his mother.

Proverbs 29:15

PARENTS

All your sons will be taught by the LORD,
and great will be your children's peace.
Isaiah 54:13

These commandments that I give you today
are to be upon your hearts. Impress them on
your children. Talk about them when you sit
at home and when you walk along the road,
when you lie down and when you get up.
Deuteronomy 6:6–7

Children's children are a crown to the aged,
and parents are the pride of their children.
Proverbs 17:6

A good man leaves an inheritance for his
children's children,
but a sinner's wealth is stored up for the
righteous.
Proverbs 13:22

The LORD said, "I have chosen him, so that
he will direct his children and his household
after him to keep the way of the LORD by
doing what is right and just."
Genesis 18:19

PATIENCE

Be joyful in hope, patient in affliction, faithful in prayer.

Romans 12:12

Be patient, then, brothers, until the Lord's coming. See how the farmer waits for the land to yield its valuable crop and how patient he is for the autumn and spring rains. You too, be patient and stand firm, because the Lord's coming is near.

James 5:7–8

Wait for the LORD;
    be strong and take heart
    and wait for the LORD.

Psalm 27:14

As for me, I watch in hope for the LORD,
    I wait for God my Savior;
    my God will hear me.

Micah 7:7

PATIENCE

I waited patiently for the LORD;
   he turned to me and heard my cry.
He lifted me out of the slimy pit,
   out of the mud and mire;
he set my feet on a rock
   and gave me a firm place to stand.

Psalm 40:1–2

A man's wisdom gives him patience;
   it is to his glory to overlook an offense.

Proverbs 19:11

A fool shows his annoyance at once,
   but a prudent man overlooks an insult.

Proverbs 12:16

A patient man has great understanding,
   but a quick-tempered man displays folly.

Proverbs 14:29

PEACE

Since we have been justified through faith, we have peace with God through our Lord Jesus Christ.

Romans 5:1

I will listen to what God the LORD will say; he promises peace to his people, his saints.

Psalm 85:8

Great peace have they who love your law, and nothing can make them stumble.

Psalm 119:165

You will keep in perfect peace him whose mind is steadfast, because he trusts in you.

Isaiah 26:3

In everything, by prayer and petition, with thanksgiving, present your requests to God. And the peace of God, which transcends all understanding, will guard your hearts and your minds in Christ Jesus.

Philippians 4:6–7

PEACE

The mind controlled by the Spirit is life and peace.

Romans 8:6

When a man's ways are pleasing to the LORD, he makes even his enemies live at peace with him.

Proverbs 16:7

Peacemakers who sow in peace raise a harvest of righteousness.

James 3:18

Jesus said, "Blessed are the peacemakers, for they will be called sons of God."

Matthew 5:9

Aim for perfection, listen to my appeal, be of one mind, live in peace. And the God of love and peace will be with you.

2 Corinthians 13:11

PERSEVERANCE

Blessed is the man who perseveres under trial, because when he has stood the test, he will receive the crown of life that God has promised to those who love him.

James 1:12

Stand firm. Let nothing move you. Always give yourselves fully to the work of the Lord, because you know that your labor in the Lord is not in vain.

1 Corinthians 15:58

Jesus said, "I am coming soon. Hold on to what you have, so that no one will take your crown."

Revelation 3:11

Be self-controlled and alert. Your enemy the devil prowls around like a roaring lion looking for someone to devour. Resist him, standing firm in the faith, because you know that your brothers throughout the world are undergoing the same kind of sufferings.

1 Peter 5:8–9

PERSEVERANCE

To those who by persistence in doing good seek glory, honor and immortality, he will give eternal life.

Romans 2:7

My steps have held to your paths;
   my feet have not slipped.

Psalm 17:5

Perseverance must finish its work so that you may be mature and complete, not lacking anything.

James 1:4–5

Let us not become weary in doing good, for at the proper time we will reap a harvest if we do not give up.

Galatians 6:9

PRAISE

Praise the LORD, O my soul,
   and forget not all his benefits—
who forgives all your sins
   and heals all your diseases.

Psalm 103:2–3

Praise be to the LORD,
   for he has heard my cry for mercy.

Psalm 28:6

I will praise you forever for what you
     have done;
   in your name I will hope, for your name
     is good.
   I will praise you in the presence of your
     saints.

Psalm 52:9

PRAISE

You turned my wailing into dancing;
  you removed my sackcloth and clothed
    me with joy,
that my heart may sing to you and not be
    silent.
  O LORD my God, I will give you
    thanks forever.

Psalm 30:11–12

I have set the LORD always before me.
  Because he is at my right hand,
  I will not be shaken.
Therefore my heart is glad and my
    tongue rejoices;
  my body also will rest secure.

Psalm 16:8–9

PRAYER

Jesus said, "If you remain in me and my words remain in you, ask whatever you wish, and it will be given you."

John 15:7

I call on you, O God, for you will answer me; give ear to me and hear my prayer.

Psalm 17:6

Jesus said, "Everyone who asks receives; he who seeks finds; and to him who knocks, the door will be opened."

Matthew 7:8

If any of you lacks wisdom, he should ask God, who gives generously to all without finding fault, and it will be given to him.

James 1:5

Jesus said, "If you believe, you will receive whatever you ask for in prayer."

Matthew 21:22

PRAYER

Jesus said, "Until now you have not asked for anything in my name. Ask and you will receive, and your joy will be complete."

John 16:24

In the same way, the Spirit helps us in our weakness. We do not know what we ought to pray for, but the Spirit himself intercedes for us with groans that words cannot express.

Romans 8:26

Jesus said, "But I tell you: Love your enemies and pray for those who persecute you, that you may be sons of your Father in heaven. He causes his sun to rise on the evil and the good, and sends rain on the righteous and the unrighteous."

Matthew 5:44–45

Pray in the Spirit on all occasions with all kinds of prayers and requests. With this in mind, be alert and always keep on praying for all the saints.

Ephesians 6:18

PRESENCE OF GOD

The LORD is near to all who call on him,
   to all who call on him in truth.

Psalm 145:18

Reach out for God and find him, though he
is not far from each one of us.

Acts 17:27

If I rise on the wings of the dawn,
   if I settle on the far side of the sea,
even there your hand will guide me,
   your right hand will hold me fast.

Psalm 139:9–10

God has said, "Never will I leave you;
   never will I forsake you."

Hebrews 13:5

Even though I walk
   through the valley of the shadow of death,
I will fear no evil,
   for you are with me;
your rod and your staff,
   they comfort me.

Psalm 23:4

PRESENCE OF GOD

———— ✦ ————

"When you pass through the waters,
  I will be with you;
and when you pass through the rivers,
  they will not sweep over you.
When you walk through the fire,
  you will not be burned;
  the flames will not set you ablaze.
For I am the LORD, your God,
  the Holy One of Israel, your Savior."

Isaiah 43:2–3

Be strong and courageous. Do not be afraid
or terrified because of them, for the LORD
your God goes with you; he will never leave
you nor forsake you.

Deuteronomy 31:6

The LORD replied, "My Presence will go
with you, and I will give you rest."

Exodus 33:14

PRIORITIES

Jesus said, "Seek first his kingdom and his righteousness, and all these things will be given to you as well."

Matthew 6:33

Now all has been heard;
*   here is the conclusion of the matter:*
Fear God and keep his commandments,
*   for this is the whole duty of man.*

Ecclesiastes 12:13

We make it our goal to please him, whether we are at home in the body or away from it.

2 Corinthians 5:9

Jesus said, "No one can serve two masters. Either he will hate the one and love the other, or he will be devoted to the one and despise the other. You cannot serve both God and Money."

Matthew 6:24

PRIORITIES

He who pursues righteousness and love
  finds life, prosperity and honor.
Proverbs 21:21

Flee the evil desires of youth, and pursue
righteousness, faith, love and peace, along
with those who call on the Lord out of a
pure heart.
2 Timothy 2:22

Like newborn babies, crave pure spiritual
milk, so that by it you may grow up in your
salvation.
1 Peter 2:2

Forgetting what is behind and straining
toward what is ahead, I press on toward the
goal to win the prize for which God has
called me heavenward in Christ Jesus.
Philippians 3:13–14

Jehoshaphat also said to the king of Israel,
"First seek the counsel of the LORD."
1 Kings 22:5

PROTECTION

Cast your cares on the LORD
    and he will sustain you;
he will never let the righteous fall.

Psalm 55:22

You are my hiding place;
    you will protect me from trouble
    and surround me with songs of deliverance.

Psalm 32:7

The LORD loves the just
    and will not forsake his faithful ones.
They will be protected forever,
    but the offspring of the wicked will be
        cut off.

Psalm 37:28

"Because he loves me," says the LORD,
       "I will rescue him;
    I will protect him, for he acknowledges
       my name.
He will call upon me, and I will answer him;
    I will be with him in trouble,
    I will deliver him and honor him."

Psalm 91:14–15

PROTECTION

The eternal God is your refuge,
   and underneath are the everlasting arms.
He will drive out your enemy before you,
   saying, "Destroy him!"

> *Deuteronomy 33:27*

As for God, his way is perfect;
   the word of the LORD is flawless.
He is a shield
   for all who take refuge in him.

> *2 Samuel 22:31*

He holds victory in store for the upright,
   he is a shield to those whose walk is
      blameless,
for he guards the course of the just
   and protects the way of his faithful ones.

> *Proverbs 2:7–8*

The LORD watches over all who love him,
   but all the wicked he will destroy.

> *Psalm 145:20*

The Lord is faithful, and he will strengthen
and protect you from the evil one.

> *2 Thessalonians 3:3*

PROVISION OF GOD

My God will meet all your needs according
to his glorious riches in Christ Jesus.

Philippians 4:19

The LORD *is my shepherd, I shall not be*
in want.

Psalm 23:1

Be glad, O people of Zion,
rejoice in the LORD *your God,*
for he has given you
the autumn rains in righteousness.
He sends you abundant showers,
both autumn and spring rains, as before.

Joel 2:23

God provides food for those who fear him;
he remembers his covenant forever.

Psalm 111:5

PROVISION OF GOD

———— ❧❧❧ ————

I will bless her with abundant provisions;
   her poor will I satisfy with food.

   Psalm 132:15

God has shown kindness by giving you rain
from heaven and crops in their seasons; he
provides you with plenty of food and fills
your hearts with joy.

   Acts 14:17

God is able to make all grace abound to you,
so that in all things at all times, having all
that you need, you will abound in every
good work.

   2 Corinthians 9:8

Jesus said, "Which of you, if his son asks for
bread, will give him a stone? Or if he asks for
a fish, will give him a snake? If you, then,
though you are evil, know how to give good
gifts to your children, how much more will
your Father in heaven give good gifts to
those who ask him!"

   Matthew 7:9–11

PURPOSE

The LORD will fulfill his purpose for me;
your love, O LORD, endures forever—
do not abandon the works of your hands.
Psalm 138:8

We know that in all things God works for the good of those who love him, who have been called according to his purpose.
Romans 8:28

We constantly pray for you, that our God may count you worthy of his calling, and that by his power he may fulfill every good purpose of yours and every act prompted by your faith.
2 Thessalonians 1:11

Do not conform any longer to the pattern of this world, but be transformed by the renewing of your mind. Then you will be able to test and approve what God's will is—his good, pleasing and perfect will.
Romans 12:2

PURPOSE

It is God's will that by doing good you should silence the ignorant talk of foolish men.

1 Peter 2:15

Everyone who confesses the name of the Lord must turn away from wickedness.... If a man cleanses himself from the latter, he will be an instrument for noble purposes, made holy, useful to the Master and prepared to do any good work.

2 Timothy 2:19, 21

We are God's workmanship, created in Christ Jesus to do good works, which God prepared in advance for us to do.

Ephesians 2:10

Because God wanted to make the unchanging nature of his purpose very clear to the heirs of what was promised, he confirmed it with an oath. God did this so that ... we who have fled to take hold of the hope offered to us may be greatly encouraged.

Hebrews 6:17–18

QUIETNESS & REST

I have stilled and quieted my soul;
　　like a weaned child with its mother,
　　like a weaned child is my soul within me.

Psalm 131:2

Be still before the LORD and wait patiently
for him.

Psalm 37:7

The Lord will fight for you; you need only to
be still.

Exodus 14:14

"Be still, and know that I am God;
　　I will be exalted among the nations,
　　I will be exalted in the earth."

Psalm 46:10

Teach me, and I will be quiet;
　　show me where I have been wrong.

Job 6:24

QUIETNESS & REST

Jesus said, "Come to me, all you who are weary and burdened, and I will give you rest. Take my yoke upon you and learn from me, for I am gentle and humble in heart, and you will find rest for your souls. For my yoke is easy and my burden is light."

Matthew 11:28–30

The fear of the LORD leads to life:
  Then one rests content, untouched by trouble.

Proverbs 19:23

I will lie down and sleep in peace,
  for you alone, O LORD,
  make me dwell in safety.

Psalm 4:8

My soul finds rest in God alone;
  my salvation comes from him.
He alone is my rock and my salvation;
  he is my fortress, I will never be shaken.

Psalm 62:1–2

REDEMPTION

Christ redeemed us from the curse of the law by becoming a curse for us, for it is written: "Cursed is everyone who is hung on a tree."

Galatians 3:13

You know that it was not with perishable things such as silver or gold that you were redeemed from the empty way of life handed down to you from your forefathers, but with the precious blood of Christ, a lamb without blemish or defect.

1 Peter 1:18–19

Christ did not enter by means of the blood of goats and calves; but he entered the Most Holy Place once for all by his own blood, having obtained eternal redemption.

Hebrews 9:12

In Jesus we have redemption through his blood, the forgiveness of sins, in accordance with the riches of God's grace.

Ephesians 1:7

REDEMPTION

It is because of him that you are in Christ
Jesus, who has become for us wisdom from
God—that is, our righteousness, holiness
and redemption.

1 Corinthians 1:30

God has rescued us from the dominion of
darkness and brought us into the kingdom of
the Son he loves, in whom we have redemption, the forgiveness of sins.

Colossians 1:13–14

You came near when I called you,
  and you said, "Do not fear."
O Lord, you took up my case;
  you redeemed my life.

Lamentations 3:57–58

"I have swept away your offenses like a cloud,
  your sins like the morning mist.
Return to me,
  for I have redeemed you," says the LORD.

Isaiah 44:22

REPENTANCE

Repent, then, and turn to God, so that your sins may be wiped out, that times of refreshing may come from the Lord.

Acts 3:19

The Lord is not slow in keeping his promise, as some understand slowness. He is patient with you, not wanting anyone to perish, but everyone to come to repentance.

2 Peter 3:9

Jesus said, "I tell you that in the same way there will be more rejoicing in heaven over one sinner who repents than over ninety-nine righteous persons who do not need to repent."

Luke 15:7

"If a wicked man turns away from all the sins he has committed and keeps all my decrees and does what is just and right, he will surely live; he will not die," says the LORD.

Ezekiel 18:21

REPENTANCE

Let the wicked forsake his way
and the evil man his thoughts.
Let him turn to the LORD, and he will have
mercy on him,
and to our God, for he will freely pardon.

Isaiah 55:7

"If my people, who are called by my name, will humble themselves and pray and seek my face and turn from their wicked ways, then will I hear from heaven and will forgive their sin and will heal their land," says the LORD.

2 Chronicles 7:14

REWARD

"I the LORD search the heart
    and examine the mind,
to reward a man according to his conduct,
    according to what his deeds deserve."

Jeremiah 17:10

The LORD has dealt with me according to
        my righteousness;
    according to the cleanness of my hands he
        has rewarded me.

Psalm 18:20

Whatever you do, work at it with all your
heart, as working for the Lord, not for men,
since you know that you will receive an
inheritance from the Lord as a reward. It is
the Lord Christ you are serving.

Colossians 3:23–24

Blessed is the man who perseveres under
trial, because when he has stood the test, he
will receive the crown of life that God has
promised to those who love him.

James 1:12

REWARD

Jesus said, "When you pray, go into your room, close the door and pray to your Father, who is unseen. Then your Father, who sees what is done in secret, will reward you."

Matthew 6:6

Fire will test the quality of each man's work. If what he has built survives, he will receive his reward.

1 Corinthians 3:13–14

Jesus said, "Love your enemies, do good to them, and lend to them without expecting to get anything back. Then your reward will be great, and you will be sons of the Most High, because he is kind to the ungrateful and wicked."

Luke 6:35

You know that the Lord will reward every-one for whatever good he does, whether he is slave or free.

Ephesians 6:8

RIGHTEOUSNESS

Jesus said,
"Blessed are those who hunger and thirst for
     righteousness,
  for they will be filled.

Matthew 5:6

Sow for yourselves righteousness,
  reap the fruit of unfailing love,
and break up your unplowed ground;
  for it is time to seek the LORD,
until he comes
  and showers righteousness on you.

Hosea 10:12

The fruit of righteousness will be peace;
  the effect of righteousness will be
     quietness and confidence forever.

Isaiah 32:17

In the way of righteousness there is life;
  along that path is immortality.

Proverbs 12:28

The eyes of the Lord are on the righteous
and his ears are attentive to their prayer.

1 Peter 3:12

RIGHTEOUSNESS

Surely he will never be shaken;
a righteous man will be remembered forever.
He will have no fear of bad news;
his heart is steadfast, trusting in the LORD.

Psalm 112:6–7

The mouth of the righteous man utters wisdom,
and his tongue speaks what is just.
The law of his God is in his heart;
his feet do not slip.

Psalm 37:30–31

He who pursues righteousness and love
finds life, prosperity and honor.

Proverbs 21:21

Religion that God our Father accepts as pure
and faultless is this: to look after orphans and
widows in their distress and to keep oneself
from being polluted by the world.

James 1:27

God does not take his eyes off the righteous;
he enthrones them with kings
and exalts them forever.

Job 36:7

SALVATION

God our Savior ... wants all men to be saved
and to come to a knowledge of the truth.

1 Timothy 2:3–4

God says,
"In the time of my favor I heard you,
and in the day of salvation I helped you."
I tell you, now is the time of God's favor,
now is the day of salvation.

2 Corinthians 6:2

If you confess with your mouth, "Jesus is
Lord," and believe in your heart that God
raised him from the dead, you will be saved.

Romans 10:9

All the prophets testify about Jesus that
everyone who believes in him receives forgiveness of sins through his name.

Acts 10:43

SALVATION

Once made perfect, Jesus became the source of eternal salvation for all who obey him.

Hebrews 5:9

Jesus said, "Whoever believes and is baptized will be saved, but whoever does not believe will be condemned."

Mark 16:16

God our Savior saved us, not because of righteous things we had done, but because of his mercy. He saved us through the washing of rebirth and renewal by the Holy Spirit.

Titus 3:5

He lifted me out of the slimy pit,
    out of the mud and mire;
he set my feet on a rock
    and gave me a firm place to stand.

Psalm 40:2

SCRIPTURE

Jesus answered, "It is written: 'Man does not live on bread alone, but on every word that comes from the mouth of God.'"

Matthew 4:4

The law of the LORD is perfect,
*   reviving the soul.*
The statutes of the LORD are trustworthy,
*   making wise the simple.*

Psalm 19:7

Everything that was written in the past was written to teach us, so that through endurance and the encouragement of the Scriptures we might have hope.

Romans 15:4

The word of God is living and active. Sharper than any double-edged sword, it penetrates even to dividing soul and spirit, joints and marrow; it judges the thoughts and attitudes of the heart.

Hebrews 4:12

Great peace have they who love your law,
*   and nothing can make them stumble.*

Psalm 119:165

SCRIPTURE

All Scripture is God-breathed and is useful for teaching, rebuking, correcting and training in righteousness, so that the man of God may be thoroughly equipped for every good work.

2 Timothy 3:16–17

The man who looks intently into the perfect law that gives freedom, and continues to do this, not forgetting what he has heard, but doing it—he will be blessed in what he does.

James 1:25

Do not let this Book of the Law depart from your mouth; meditate on it day and night, so that you may be careful to do everything written in it. Then you will be prosperous and successful.

Joshua 1:8

If you pay attention to these laws and are careful to follow them, then the LORD your God will keep his covenant of love with you, as he swore to your forefathers.

Deuteronomy 7:12

SECURITY

LORD, you have assigned me my portion
    and my cup;
    you have made my lot secure.

Psalm 16:5

"I will heal my people and will let them enjoy
abundant peace and security," says the LORD.

Jeremiah 33:6

Jesus said, "I give them eternal life, and they
shall never perish; no one can snatch them
out of my hand."

John 10:28

Those who know your name will trust in you,
    for you, LORD, have never forsaken those
        who seek you.

Psalm 9:10

Those who trust in the LORD are like
    Mount Zion,
    which cannot be shaken but endures forever.

Psalm 125:1

SECURITY

I have set the LORD always before me.
   Because he is at my right hand,
   I will not be shaken.

Psalm 16:8

Let the beloved of the LORD rest secure in him,
for he shields him all day long, and the one the
LORD loves rests between his shoulders.

Deuteronomy 33:12

We say with confidence,
   "The Lord is my helper; I will not be afraid.
   What can man do to me?"

Hebrews 13:6

I am convinced that neither death nor life,
neither angels nor demons, neither the present nor the future, nor any powers, neither
height nor depth, nor anything else in all
creation, will be able to separate us from the
love of God that is in Christ Jesus our Lord.

Romans 8:38–39

Who is going to harm you if you are eager to
do good?

1 Peter 3:13

SEEKING GOD

Seek the LORD while he may be found;
call on him while he is near.
Let the wicked forsake his way
and the evil man his thoughts.
Let him turn to the LORD, and he will
have mercy on him,
and to our God, for he will freely pardon.
Isaiah 55:6–7

"You will call upon me and come and pray to
me, and I will listen to you. You will seek me
and find me when you seek me with all your
heart. I will be found by you," declares the LORD.
Jeremiah 29:12–14

Jesus says to you, "Ask and it will be given to
you; seek and you will find; knock and the
door will be opened to you. For everyone
who asks receives; he who seeks finds; and to
him who knocks, the door will be opened."
Luke 11:9–10

Jesus said, "Seek God's kingdom, and these
things will be given to you as well."
Luke 12:31

SEEKING GOD

Without faith it is impossible to please God, because anyone who comes to him must believe that he exists and that he rewards those who earnestly seek him.

Hebrews 11:6

The LORD is good to those whose hope is in him, to the one who seeks him.

Lamentations 3:25

*The LORD looks down from heaven
   on the sons of men
to see if there are any who understand,
   any who seek God.*

Psalm 14:2

*Those who know your name will trust in you,
   for you, LORD, have never forsaken those
      who seek you.*

Psalm 9:10

If ... you seek the LORD your God, you will find him if you look for him with all your heart and with all your soul.

Deuteronomy 4:29

SELF-CONTROL

Jesus said to his disciples, "If anyone would come after me, he must deny himself and take up his cross and follow me."

Matthew 16:24

The grace of God that brings salvation has appeared to all men. It teaches us to say "No" to ungodliness and worldly passions, and to live self-controlled, upright and godly lives in this present age.

Titus 2:11–12

Prepare your minds for action; be self-controlled; set your hope fully on the grace to be given you when Jesus Christ is revealed.

1 Peter 1:13

The end of all things is near. Therefore be clear minded and self-controlled so that you can pray.

1 Peter 4:7

Let us be self-controlled, putting on faith and love as a breastplate, and the hope of salvation as a helmet.

1 Thessalonians 5:8

SELF-CONTROL

Jesus said, "Watch and pray so that you will not fall into temptation. The spirit is willing, but the body is weak."

Matthew 26:41

Be self-controlled and alert. Your enemy the devil prowls around like a roaring lion looking for someone to devour.

1 Peter 5:8

If you live according to the sinful nature, you will die; but if by the Spirit you put to death the misdeeds of the body, you will live.

Romans 8:13

No temptation has seized you except what is common to man. And God is faithful; he will not let you be tempted beyond what you can bear. But when you are tempted, he will also provide a way out so that you can stand up under it.

1 Corinthians 10:13

Because Christ himself suffered when he was tempted, he is able to help those who are being tempted.

Hebrews 2:18

SELF-WORTH

"Before I formed you in the womb I knew you,
　　before you were born I set you apart,"
　　　says the LORD.

Jeremiah 1:5

Jesus said, "Are not two sparrows sold for a penny? Yet not one of them will fall to the ground apart from the will of your Father. And even the very hairs of your head are all numbered. So don't be afraid; you are worth more than many sparrows."

Matthew 10:29–31

"Since you are precious and honored in my
　　sight,
　　and because I love you,
I will give men in exchange for you,
　　and people in exchange for your life,"
　　　says the LORD.

Isaiah 43:4

Know that the LORD is God.
　　It is he who made us, and we are his;
　　we are his people, the sheep of his pasture.

Psalm 100:3

SELF-WORTH

You created my inmost being;
*   you knit me together in my mother's womb.*
I praise you because I am fearfully and
*   wonderfully made;*
*   your works are wonderful,*
*   I know that full well.*

Psalm 139:13–14

"Can a mother forget the baby at her breast
*   and have no compassion on the child she*
*   has borne?*
Though she may forget,
*   I will not forget you!*
See, I have engraved you on the palms of
*   my hands;*
*   your walls are ever before me," says the* LORD.

Isaiah 49:15–16

God predestined us to be adopted as his sons
through Jesus Christ, in accordance with his
pleasure and will—to the praise of his glorious grace, which he has freely given us in
the One he loves.

Ephesians 1:5–6

SINGLENESS

God sets the lonely in families,
    he leads forth the prisoners with singing;
    but the rebellious live in a sun-scorched
        land.

Psalm 68:6

Jesus said, "Surely I am with you always, to
the very end of the age."

Matthew 28:20

Yet I am always with you, O LORD;
    you hold me by my right hand.

Psalm 73:23

I will betroth you to me forever;
    I will betroth you in righteousness and
        justice,
    in love and compassion.
I will betroth you in faithfulness,
    and you will acknowledge the LORD.

Hosea 2:19–20

To the unmarried and the widows I say: It is
good for them to stay unmarried, as I am.

1 Corinthians 7:8

SINGLENESS

Your Maker is your husband—
  the Lord Almighty is his name—
the Holy One of Israel is your Redeemer;
  he is called the God of all the earth.

Isaiah 54:5

I would like you to be free from concern. An unmarried man is concerned about the Lord's affairs—how he can please the Lord.

1 Corinthians 7:32

An unmarried woman or virgin is concerned about the Lord's affairs: Her aim is to be devoted to the Lord in both body and spirit. But a married woman is concerned about the affairs of this world—how she can please her husband. I am saying this for your own good, not to restrict you, but that you may live in a right way in undivided devotion to the Lord.

1 Corinthians 7:34–35

SPEECH

He who guards his mouth and his tongue
keeps himself from calamity.

Proverbs 21:23

We all stumble in many ways. If anyone is
never at fault in what he says, he is a perfect
man, able to keep his whole body in check.
When we put bits into the mouths of horses
to make them obey us, we can turn the
whole animal.

James 3:2–3

Do not let any unwholesome talk come out
of your mouths, but only what is helpful for
building others up according to their needs,
that it may benefit those who listen.

Ephesians 4:29

A gentle answer turns away wrath.

Proverbs 15:1

Whoever would love life and see good days
must keep his tongue from evil and his lips
from deceitful speech.

1 Peter 3:10

SPEECH

The tongue that brings healing is a tree of life,
  but a deceitful tongue crushes the spirit.
                                    Proverbs 15:4

Speaking the truth in love, we will in all
things grow up into him who is the Head,
that is, Christ.
                                    Ephesians 4:15

Pleasant words are a honeycomb,
  sweet to the soul and healing to the bones.
                                    Proverbs 16:24

A word aptly spoken
  is like apples of gold in settings of silver.
                                    Proverbs 25:11

The quiet words of the wise are more to be
      heeded
  than the shouts of a ruler of fools.
                                    Ecclesiastes 9:17

STABILITY

I have set the LORD *always before me.*
Because he is at my right hand,
I will not be shaken.

Psalm 16:8

If the LORD *delights in a man's way,*
he makes his steps firm;
though he stumble, he will not fall,
for the LORD *upholds him with his hand.*

Psalm 37:23–24

My soul finds rest in God alone;
my salvation comes from him.
He alone is my rock and my salvation;
he is my fortress, I will never be shaken.

Psalm 62:1–2

The God of all grace, who called you to his
eternal glory in Christ, after you have suffered a little while, will himself restore you
and make you strong, firm and steadfast.

1 Peter 5:10

The man of integrity walks securely,
but he who takes crooked paths will be
found out.

Proverbs 10:9

STABILITY

To him who is able to keep you from falling and to present you before his glorious presence without fault and with great joy—to the only God our Savior be glory, majesty, power and authority, through Jesus Christ our Lord, before all ages, now and forevermore! Amen.

Jude 1:24–25

You, O LORD, have delivered my soul from death,
my eyes from tears,
my feet from stumbling,
that I may walk before the LORD
in the land of the living.

Psalm 116:8–9

Whoever loves his brother lives in the light, and there is nothing in him to make him stumble.

1 John 2:10

Strengthen the feeble hands,
steady the knees that give way;
say to those with fearful hearts,
"Be strong, do not fear;
your God will come."

Isaiah 35:3–4

STRENGTH

"Do not fear, for I am with you;
　do not be dismayed, for I am your God.
I will strengthen you and help you;
　I will uphold you with my righteous right
　　hand."

Isaiah 41:10

I can do everything through him who gives
me strength.

Philippians 4:13

But Jesus said to me, "My grace is sufficient
for you, for my power is made perfect in
weakness." Therefore I will boast all the
more gladly about my weaknesses, so that
Christ's power may rest on me.

2 Corinthians 12:9

My flesh and my heart may fail,
　but God is the strength of my heart
　and my portion forever.

Psalm 73:26

STRENGTH

It is God who arms me with strength
*   and makes my way perfect.*
He makes my feet like the feet of a deer;
*   he enables me to stand on the heights.*

2 Samuel 22:33–34

"I will search for the lost and bring back
the strays. I will bind up the injured and
strengthen the weak, but the sleek and the
strong I will destroy. I will shepherd the
flock with justice," declares the LORD.

Ezekiel 34:16

The LORD gives strength to the weary
*   and increases the power of the weak.*

Isaiah 40:29

The LORD gives strength to his people;
*   the LORD blesses his people with peace.*

Psalm 29:11

The LORD is my strength and my song;
*   he has become my salvation.*
He is my God, and I will praise him,
*   my father's God, and I will exalt him.*

Exodus 15:2

STRENGTH

Why do you say, O Jacob,
  and complain, O Israel,
"My way is hidden from the LORD;
  my cause is disregarded by my God"?
Do you not know?
  Have you not heard?
The LORD is the everlasting God,
  the Creator of the ends of the earth.
He will not grow tired or weary,
  and his understanding no one can fathom.
He gives strength to the weary
  and increases the power of the weak.
Even youths grow tired and weary,
  and young men stumble and fall;
but those who hope in the LORD
  will renew their strength.
They will soar on wings like eagles;
  they will run and not grow weary,
  they will walk and not be faint.

Isaiah 40:27–31

STRENGTH

May God strengthen your hearts so that you
will be blameless and holy in the presence of
our God and Father when our Lord Jesus
comes with all his holy ones.

1 Thessalonians 3:13

God is our refuge and strength,
  an ever-present help in trouble.

Psalm 46:1

I will sing of your strength,
  in the morning I will sing of your love;
for you are my fortress,
  my refuge in times of trouble.

Psalm 59:16

THANKFULNESS

Let the word of Christ dwell in you richly as you teach and admonish one another with all wisdom, and as you sing psalms, hymns and spiritual songs with gratitude in your hearts to God.

Colossians 3:16

Let them give thanks to the LORD for his
*   unfailing love*
* and his wonderful deeds for men,*
for he satisfies the thirsty
* and fills the hungry with good things.*

Psalm 107:8–9

Just as you received Christ Jesus as Lord, continue to live in him, rooted and built up in him, strengthened in the faith as you were taught, and overflowing with thankfulness.

Colossians 2:6–7

Since we are receiving a kingdom that cannot be shaken, let us be thankful, and so worship God acceptably with reverence and awe.

Hebrews 12:28

THANKFULNESS

You turned my wailing into dancing;
*   you removed my sackcloth and clothed*
*   me with joy,*
that my heart may sing to you and not be
*   silent.*
*   O LORD my God, I will give you*
*   thanks forever.*

Psalm 30:11–12

Give thanks to the LORD, for he is good;
*   his love endures forever.*

1 Chronicles 16:34

The LORD is my strength and my shield;
*   my heart trusts in him, and I am helped.*
My heart leaps for joy
*   and I will give thanks to him in song.*

Psalm 28:7

Give thanks in all circumstances, for this is
God's will for you in Christ Jesus.

1 Thessalonians 5:18

THOUGHTS

Finally, brothers, whatever is true, whatever is noble, whatever is right, whatever is pure, whatever is lovely, whatever is admirable—if anything is excellent or praiseworthy—think about such things.

Philippians 4:8

Be transformed by the renewing of your mind. Then you will be able to test and approve what God's will is—his good, pleasing and perfect will.

Romans 12:2

We demolish arguments and every pretension that sets itself up against the knowledge of God, and we take captive every thought to make it obedient to Christ.

2 Corinthians 10:5

The mind controlled by the Spirit is life and peace.

Romans 8:6

THOUGHTS

The plans of the righteous are just,
    but the advice of the wicked is deceitful.

Proverbs 12:5

The LORD knows the thoughts of man;
    he knows that they are futile.

Psalm 94:11

You will keep in perfect peace
    him whose mind is steadfast,
    because he trusts in you.

Isaiah 26:3

"I the LORD search the heart
    and examine the mind,
to reward a man according to his conduct,
    according to what his deeds deserve."

Jeremiah 17:10

Jesus said,
"Blessed are the pure in heart,
    for they will see God."

Matthew 5:8

TRUST

It is better to take refuge in the LORD
*   than to trust in man.*

Psalm 118:8

Jesus said, "Trust in God; trust also in me."

John 14:1

Blessed is the man
*   who makes the LORD his trust,*
who does not look to the proud,
*   to those who turn aside to false gods.*

Psalm 40:4

This is what the Sovereign Lord, the Holy
One of Israel, says:
*   "In repentance and rest is your salvation,*
*   in quietness and trust is your strength."*

Isaiah 30:15

This is what the Sovereign Lord says:
"See, I lay a stone in Zion,
*   a tested stone,*
a precious cornerstone for a sure foundation;
*   the one who trusts will never be dismayed."*

Isaiah 28:16

TRUST

You will keep in perfect peace
    him whose mind is steadfast,
    because he trusts in you.
Trust in the LORD forever,
    for the LORD, the LORD, is the Rock eternal.

Isaiah 26:3–4

Blessed is the man who trusts in the LORD,
    whose confidence is in him.
He will be like a tree planted by the water
    that sends out its roots by the stream.
It does not fear when heat comes;
    its leaves are always green.
It has no worries in a year of drought
    and never fails to bear fruit.

Jeremiah 17:7–8

TRUTH

Kings take pleasure in honest lips;
   they value a man who speaks the truth.
Proverbs 16:13

The LORD is near to all who call on him,
   to all who call on him in truth.
Psalm 145:18

Jesus answered, "I am the way and the truth
and the life. No one comes to the Father
except through me."
John 14:6

Jesus said, ""If you hold to my teaching, you
are really my disciples. Then you will know
the truth, and the truth will set you free."
John 8:31–32

We know also that the Son of God has come
and has given us understanding, so that we
may know him who is true. And we are in
him who is true—even in his Son Jesus
Christ. He is the true God and eternal life.
1 John 5:20

TRUTH

Jesus said, "When he, the Spirit of truth, comes, he will guide you into all truth. He will not speak on his own; he will speak only what he hears, and he will tell you what is yet to come."

John 16:13

Buy the truth and do not sell it;
    get wisdom, discipline and understanding.

Proverbs 23:23

All your words are true;
    all your righteous laws are eternal.

Psalm 119:160

Joshua said, "I am about to go the way of all the earth. You know with all your heart and soul that not one of all the good promises the LORD your God gave you has failed. Every promise has been fulfilled; not one has failed."

Joshua 23:14

VICTORY

Thanks be to God! He gives us the victory through our Lord Jesus Christ.

1 Corinthians 15:57

Jesus said, "I have told you these things, so that in me you may have peace. In this world you will have trouble. But take heart! I have overcome the world."

John 16:33

Everyone born of God overcomes the world. This is the victory that has overcome the world, even our faith. Who is it that overcomes the world? Only he who believes that Jesus is the Son of God.

1 John 5:4–5

The God of peace will soon crush Satan under your feet. The grace of our Lord Jesus be with you.

Romans 16:20

With God we will gain the victory,
and he will trample down our enemies.

Psalm 60:12

VICTORY

You, dear children, are from God and have overcome them, because the one who is in you is greater than the one who is in the world.

1 John 4:4

In all these things we are more than conquerors through him who loved us.

Romans 8:37

When the perishable has been clothed with the imperishable, and the mortal with immortality, then the saying that is written will come true: "Death has been swallowed up in victory."

1 Corinthians 15:54

There is no wisdom, no insight, no plan
that can succeed against the LORD.
The horse is made ready for the day of battle,
but victory rests with the LORD.

Proverbs 21:30–31

For lack of guidance a nation falls,
but many advisers make victory sure.

Proverbs 11:14

WILL OF GOD

The world and its desires pass away, but the man who does the will of God lives forever.

1 John 2:17

Be transformed by the renewing of your mind. Then you will be able to test and approve what God's will is—his good, pleasing and perfect will.

Romans 12:2

God made known to us the mystery of his will according to his good pleasure, which he purposed in Christ, to be put into effect when the times will have reached their fulfillment—to bring all things in heaven and on earth together under one head, even Christ.

Ephesians 1:9–10

Grace and peace to you from God our Father and the Lord Jesus Christ, who gave himself for our sins to rescue us from the present evil age, according to the will of our God and Father, to whom be glory for ever and ever. Amen.

Galatians 1:3–5

WILL OF GOD

In him we were also chosen, having been predestined according to the plan of him who works out everything in conformity with the purpose of his will, in order that we, who were the first to hope in Christ, might be for the praise of his glory.

Ephesians 1:11–12

Jesus said, "My Father's will is that everyone who looks to the Son and believes in him shall have eternal life, and I will raise him up at the last day."

John 6:40

It is God's will that you should be sanctified: that you should avoid sexual immorality; that each of you should learn to control his own body in a way that is holy and honorable.

1 Thessalonians 4:3–4

It is God's will that by doing good you should silence the ignorant talk of foolish men.

1 Peter 2:15

You ought to say, "If it is the Lord's will, we will live and do this or that."

James 4:15

WISDOM

The fear of the LORD is the beginning of wisdom;
all who follow his precepts have good
understanding.
To him belongs eternal praise.

Psalm 111:10

The foolishness of God is wiser than man's
wisdom, and the weakness of God is stronger
than man's strength.

1 Corinthians 1:25

If any of you lacks wisdom, he should ask
God, who gives generously to all without
finding fault, and it will be given to him.

James 1:5

Wisdom is supreme; therefore get wisdom.
Though it cost all you have, get
understanding.

Proverbs 4:7

Know also that wisdom is sweet to your soul;
if you find it, there is a future hope for you,
and your hope will not be cut off.

Proverbs 24:14

WISDOM

Wisdom, like an inheritance, is a good thing
   and benefits those who see the sun.
Wisdom is a shelter
   as money is a shelter,
but the advantage of knowledge is this:
   that wisdom preserves the life of its possessor.
Ecclesiastes 7:11–12

How much better to get wisdom than gold,
   to choose understanding rather than silver!
Proverbs 16:16

Wisdom makes one wise man more powerful
   than ten rulers in a city.
Ecclesiastes 7:19

The wisdom that comes from heaven is first
of all pure; then peace-loving, considerate,
submissive, full of mercy and good fruit,
impartial and sincere.

James 3:17

Who is like the wise man?
   Who knows the explanation of things?
Wisdom brightens a man's face
   and changes its hard appearance.

Ecclesiastes 8:1

WITNESSING

*How beautiful on the mountains
    are the feet of those who bring good news,
who proclaim peace,
    who bring good tidings,
    who proclaim salvation,
who say to Zion,
    "Your God reigns!"*

Isaiah 52:7

Jesus came to them and said, "All authority in heaven and on earth has been given to me. Therefore go and make disciples of all nations, baptizing them in the name of the Father and of the Son and of the Holy Spirit, and teaching them to obey everything I have commanded you. And surely I am with you always, to the very end of the age."

Matthew 28:18–20

Jesus said to them, "Go into all the world and preach the good news to all creation."

Mark 16:15

WITNESSING

It is written: "I believed; therefore I have spoken." With that same spirit of faith we also believe and therefore speak.

2 Corinthians 4:13

We proclaim Christ, admonishing and teaching everyone with all wisdom, so that we may present everyone perfect in Christ.

Colossians 1:28

Do this with gentleness and respect, keeping a clear conscience, so that those who speak maliciously against your good behavior in Christ may be ashamed of their slander.

1 Peter 3:15–16

Jesus said, "In the same way, let your light shine before men, that they may see your good deeds and praise your Father in heaven."

Matthew 5:16

Jesus said, "This gospel of the kingdom will be preached in the whole world as a testimony to all nations, and then the end will come."

Matthew 24:14

WORK

Jesus said, "Do not work for food that spoils, but for food that endures to eternal life, which the Son of Man will give you. On him God the Father has placed his seal of approval."

John 6:27

Stand firm. Let nothing move you. Always give yourselves fully to the work of the Lord, because you know that your labor in the Lord is not in vain.

1 Corinthians 15:58

Never be lacking in zeal, but keep your spiritual fervor, serving the Lord.

Romans 12:11

Our people must learn to devote themselves to doing what is good, in order that they may provide for daily necessities and not live unproductive lives.

Titus 3:14

WORK

I realized that it is good and proper for a man to eat and drink, and to find satisfaction in his toilsome labor under the sun during the few days of life God has given him—for this is his lot.

Ecclesiastes 5:18

Diligent hands bring wealth.

Proverbs 10:4

The desires of the diligent are fully satisfied.

Proverbs 13:4

The sleep of a laborer is sweet,
    whether he eats little or much,
but the abundance of a rich man
    permits him no sleep.

Ecclesiastes 5:12

There remains, then, a Sabbath-rest for the people of God; for anyone who enters God's rest also rests from his own work, just as God did from his.

Hebrews 4:9–10

Look for these and other Inspirio gift
books and Zondervan Bibles at your local
Christian bookstore!

**God's Words of Life from the
Women's Devotional Bible 2**
ISBN: 0-310-97367-8

**God's Words of Life from
the NIV Men's Devotional Bible**
ISBN: 0-310-97368-6

The Student Bible
New International Version
ISBN: 0-310-92665-3

Women's Devotional Bible 2
New International Version
ISBN: 0-310-91842-1

Men's Devotional Bible
New International Version
ISBN: 0-310-91585-6

Inspire others with encouraging thoughts
from bestselling devotional Bibles and
selected Scripture verses in Inspirio's
series of topically formatted gift books.
These beautiful gift books are sure to
uplift you or someone you love.

At Inspirio we love to hear from you—
your stories, your feedback,
and your product ideas.
Please send your comments to us
by way of e-mail at
icares@zondervan.com
or to the address below:

ɣ
inspirio™

Attn: Inspirio Cares
5300 Patterson Avenue SE
Grand Rapids, MI 49530

If you would like further information
about Inspirio and the products we
create please visit us at:
www.inspiriogifts.com

Thank you and God bless!